Southern Tier
Volume One

Arch Merrill's New York

A River Ramble
The Lakes Country
The Ridge
The Towpath
Rochester Sketch Book
Stagecoach Towns
Tomahawks and Old Lace
Land of the Senecas
Upstate Echoes
Slim Fingers Beckon
Shadows on the Wall
Southern Tier – Volume I
Southern Tier – Volume II
The White Woman and Her Valley
Our Goodly Heritage
Pioneer Profiles
Bloomers and Bugles
Gaslights and Gingerbread
Fame in Our Time
Down the Lore Lanes
The Underground
The Changing Years
From Pumpkin Hook to Dumpling Hill

Southern Tier
Volume One

by
Arch Merrill

Twelfth of a Series

Empire State Books
Interlaken, New York

Library of Congress Cataloging-in-Publication Data
Merrill, Arch.
　Southern tier.

　(Arch Merrill's New York)
　Reprint. Originally published: Rochester, N.Y. :
Creek Books, 1953.
　1. New York (State)--History, Local.　I. Title.
II. Series: Merrill, Arch. New York.
F124.M55　1986　　　　　　974.7　　　　　　86-7694
ISBN 0-932334-46-6

First published by the author in 1953
Reprinted by Creek Books
Reprinted by Empire State Books
June 1986 — 3000 copies.

ISBN: 0-932334-46-6
Manufactured in the United States

A *quality* publication of
**Heart of the Lakes Publishing
Interlaken, New York 14847**

Arch Merrill

Without his small town upbringing, Arch Merrill might never have possessed the folksy touch that we associate with his writing. Born in the Cattaraugus County community of Sandusky (nicknamed Henpeck), he briefly attended high school in Buffalo, 45 miles away, before graduating from nearby Arcade High School.

He attended Hobart College in Geneva for a year, then saw service with the Army Engineers in France in World War I, joining the *Rochester Democrat and Chronicle* for the first time upon discharge. He married Katherine M. Towell of Rushford, Allegany County, in 1923; they had one daughter, Marion.

Merrill's entry into journalism came as a youth when he wrote social notes for the *Buffalo Evening News*. But it was his experience at William Randolph Hearst's short-lived *Rochester Journal-American*, between stints at the *Democrat and Chronicle*, that forged the spare, unpretentious prose style that became the hallmark of his 23 popular histories.

Merrill always regarded his books as secondary to his main calling—journalism. Seemingly effortlessly, he poured out most of them early in the morning after the *Democrat and Chronicle* had been put to bed, where he was night City Editor. A congenial man with a powerful memory, Merrill moulded several generations of young newspapermen in his rigorous standards of accuracy. I was fortunate enough to have been one of them.

Mitchell Kaidy
Rochester
April 1986

Contents

1. Four Western Counties — 3
2. Chautauqua, County of Grapes and Culture — 7
3. Silver Creek, Northern Gateway — 10
4. Dunkirk, Generous and Gusty — 14
5. Fredonia—Traditions, Tourists and Teachers — 22
6. Vineyard Villages—Brocton, Westfield, Ripley — 30
7. Lily Dale, "Voices from Beyond" — 42
8. Chautauqua Lake, "Bag Tied in the Middle" — 46
9. Citadel of Culture — 53
10. The Town That James Built — 60
11. Cattaraugus, High, Wide and Handsome — 68
12. Olean and Oil — 70
13. Salamanca and Senecas — 85
14. In the "Hills of Home" — 97
15. Allegany, "Roof of the Tier" — 111
16. River-Canal Towns — 114
17. Philip Church's Old Domain — 124
18. Named for a Saxon King — 133
19. Wellsville and the Oil Country — 142
20. Old "Stew-ben" — 156
21. Where Potato Is King — 158
22. Of Wine and Wings — 168
23. Bath, the Grand Dame — 178
24. Indomitable Hornell — 187
25. The Painted Post — 194
26. Corning, the Crystal City — 199

List of Illustrations

	FACING PAGE
Twilight at Chautauqua—Palestine Park and Miller Bell Tower	22
Chautauqua Institution's Hall of Philosophy	23
Lake Erie's Rugged Shore near Dunkirk	38
"Three Sisters" at Rock City near Olean	39
Red House Lake in Allegany State Park	86
"Garbage Collector" in Allegany State Park	87
Oil Spurts High Over Derrick near Richburg	102
Wellsville's "Pink House"	103
Alfred's Carillon, Oldest in America	150
Grape Harvest Along Keuka Lake	151
Craftsman in Crystal at Corning	166
Biggest Piece of Glass Ever Cast, on Exhibit at Corning Glass Center	167

SOUTHERN TIER

Chapter 1

Four Western Counties

Look at a New York State map—not a road map but one that shows the county lines—and you will note a row of seven counties with a common southern boundary, the straight, undeviating line which separates New York from Pennsylvania.

Those seven counties, reading west to east, are Chautauqua, Cattaraugus, Allegany, Steuben, Chemung, Tioga and Broome. They make up the Southern Tier.

This book, the first of two on the Southern Tier, covers the four western counties. I was born in one of them, Cattaraugus, and to me the "Tier" is the "hills of home." Once a hillbilly always a hillbilly.

The Southern Tier is rugged country. In the North the foothills of the Alleghenies are rolling. In the South they become mountains, although those who live in them are content to call them "hills." About the only level stretch in the Southern Tier is that narrow, fertile strip along capricious old Lake Erie which produces more grapes than any other region in the state. But even there the cliffs that surround the sandy beaches are rough and rugged.

History has been made in "the hills of home." From the towering ridges once blazed the signal fires of the Indians—the Eries and their conquerors, the Senecas, when all the land was theirs. Then the white man came and answered the challenge of the hills. He built his roads along narrow old

Indian trails. He cleared the land and reared his cabins, even on the highest peaks. He even dug canals through the stony uplands. And he built the longest railroad in the world, bit by bit, through the formidable hills to tie together the communities of the Southern Tier and end their commercial isolation.

Things never came easy for the Southern Tier. Its very climate is challenging and breeds a hardy people. The white man not only conquered the hills but he drew from their rocky depths buried treasure, oil, the liquid gold that is the prize of empire. Today Allegany and Cattaraugus Counties produce the bulk of New York State's petroleum and much of her natural gas.

Vineyards flourish on steep and sunny slopes around Keuka Lake. Potatoes grow on plateaus 2,000 feet above sea level. There are "cattle upon a thousand hills," for the Southern Tier is a great dairying section.

Nearly 350,000 people live in the four western counties, 125,000 of them in the five industrial cities, Jamestown, Olean, Dunkirk, Corning, Hornell and Salamanca. There are brisk villages that are veritable cities, such as oil-affluent Wellsville, historic Fredonia and stately Bath.

In the industrial cities live people of many bloods. In the rural regions the people are mostly of the old stock that settled the land. They are hereditary Republicans and overcome any Democratic swing in the cities. And on two reservations, a tiny remnant of their old empire, are huddled a few hundred Senecas, once the proud "Keepers of the Western Door."

In the western counties there are three institutions of higher learning, a state teachers' college and the world-known Chautauqua Institution, for 80 Summers a citadel of popular education.

Nature molded this land with a bold and lavish hand. The ever majestic wooded hills blaze with a multi-colored glory in the Autumn. The lazy winding rivers, the Allegheny, the Genesee, the Cattaraugus, the Conhocton, the Chemung, the Canaseraga, the Canisteo, became raging torrents in the Spring.

Millions of years ago, the retreating Ice Age left wonders in its wake, acres of weirdly shaped boulders with "streets" winding through them, like the fabulous Rock City near Olean and the Panama Rocks near Chautauqua Lake. And there is "a well that breathes" and a road that gives you the impression you are traveling downhill when you are actually going up.

For all its spectacles and wonders, the Southern Tier basically is the land of the familiar things, the land of the robin and the maple tree, of the lilac bush by the door and the statue of the Civil War soldier in the public square, of the Queen Anne's lace in the fields of Summer and the hunters and the deer thick in the woods of Fall. When I was a boy, it was a land of cheese factories at nearly every crossroads and almost every maple grove was a "sugar bush." But they are fading fast away.

Common interests transcend governmental boundary lines. The Southern Tier is far flung and doubtless Jamestown, city of Swedes and hills, has more in common with its neighbor, Warren, just over the Pennsylvania line, than it has with Corning, the Crystal City, far to the eastward. But both Jamestown and Corning are governed from Albany and not from Harrisburg. And the cities of the Southern Tier are bound together also by the Erie Railroad, Route 17 and the rivalry of the PONY League.

The residents of the Southern Tier, I found, have the common traits of friendliness and co-operation. I am grateful to all the librarians, the editors, the public relations and

Chamber of Commerce officials who helped me gather material for this book.

Particularly I would like to acknowledge the aid given by: Miss Maud D. Brooks, Olean city historian; Father Ireneaus Herscher, OFM, librarian of St. Bonaventure University; Dr. Stephen W. Paine, president of Houghton College; Dean Fred H. Gertz of Alfred University and Milo Van Hall and Mrs. Helen Cottrell of the Alfred Agricultural-Technical Institute; Hubert D. Bliss and Mrs. Bliss of the *Wellsville Democrat;* H. R. Helsby, editor of the *Olean Times-Herald;* Latham B. Weber of the *Salamanca Republican-Press;* Robert Aldrich of the *Randolph Register;* Raymond V. Carroll, Ellicottville town historian; Mrs. Ida M. Sager, Cattaraugus village historian; Robert Galloway of Silver Creek, counsel for the Seneca Republic; Mrs. Margaret Weimer of the *Fredonia Censor;* Mayor Francis P. Hogan of Hornell; Steuben County Clerk R. B. Oldfield of Bath and William Stempfle of Bath.

I drew heavily on the comprehensive volume *Empire Oil* by John P. Herrick of Olean and Los Angeles, for material on the Southern Tier oil industry.

For all the way from Barcelona on the west, where the fishing fleets still spread their nets in Lake Erie's waters, to the square at Painted Post on the east where the bronze Indian chief stretches out a hand of welcome, I found the people of the Southern Tier generous and helpful to the stranger in their midst.

Chapter 2

Chautauqua, County of Grapes and Culture

Chautauqua is an old Indian name. It is the name of the most westerly county of the Empire State, which, when it was created in 1808, took the name of the big blue lake in its heart. Until 1849 the official spelling was *Chautauque*.

It is a name known in far corners of the world and one that has found its way into the dictionaries—because of the Chautauqua lyceum circuits which borrowed the name of an old cultural, religious assembly on the shore of the inland lake and pitched their brown tents along hundreds of Main Streets in the hinterlands during the first quarter of this century.

There are several translations of the old Indian word. Chautauqua variously means "bag tied in the middle," which refers to the hour-glass shape of the lake; "where the fish was taken out," because of a big legendary "muskie" which after being caught by Indians leaped out of their canoe back into the lake, and "the place of easy death." That last rather doleful version is woven around the legend of an Indian maid who, after eating a root which created a tormenting thirst, stooped to drink of the waters of the lake and disappeared in its depths.

Chautauqua is rich in history. From Barcelona on Lake Erie, over the ridge that divides the waters, to Chautauqua Lake ran a well-marked Indian trail, the portage for the war canoes. It was the highway of the Eries, the "People of the

Cat," before their warlike kinsmen, the Senecas, "The People of the Hill," took over the domain in bloody warfare at mid-17th Century. It may have been in Chautauqua that the decisive battle was fought, in which the Senecas, using their canoes, first as shields and then as scaling ladders, seized the last stronghold of the Eries.

In 1749 French soldiers under De Celoron followed the portage trail as they swung over the hills and down the waterways, claiming the land for France. Four years later the French built a wagon road on the old trail. It was the first white man's project in the Southern Tier. Today the white man's motor highway, Route 17, follows that same old trail.

Chautauqua is the leading grape-growing county in the state. The vineyards cover a narrow 40-mile stretch along Lake Erie, a level countryside unlike the rest of the Southern Tier. West of the grape belt, which produces much grape juice and little wine, is a chain of rugged hills. It is the divide which also stretches across Northern Cattaraugus County. It is said that rain falling on one side of an old barn on the dividing ridge in Chautauqua County finds its way into Lake Erie while the drops that fall on the other side of the barn reach the Gulf of Mexico.

In the interior the hills roll up to an elevation of more than 1,700 feet in the Gerry-Cherry Creek area. They are mighty along the state line, too. The hill country is dairying country. The scenery is pastoral and the people are mostly old pioneer stock.

In Chautauqua are two industrial cities, Jamestown on her hills and Dunkirk on Lake Erie. Jamestown's population is heavily Swedish. Dunkirk has a large Polish colony. Around Silver Creek and in the vineyard belt are many of Italian blood. Chautauqua's ethnic pattern is checkered.

This is the most complex and sophisticated, as well as the

most populous (135,189) of the four western counties. Tourists on three great highways know Chautauqua County. For 80 years thousands have been storming the golden gate of learning at the Chautauqua Institution's assembly grounds.

In this remarkable county, there is another assembly. In the green and wooded hills around the Cassadaga Lakes is Lily Dale, the Spiritualist center where are heard voices **not** of this world.

Chapter 3

Silver Creek, Northern Gateway

Silver Creek, an unpretentious village of 3,000 with a pleasing name, is on the shore of Lake Erie, on the fringe of the Cattaraugus Indian Reservation and is the northern gateway to the lush Chautauqua fruit belt.

Until recently Silver Creek could claim the busiest crossroads, traffic wise, in any Upstate village.

Once the "biggest tree in the world" grew there.

Off its shore occurred the greatest of Lake Erie's maritime disasters.

Its "skew arch" railroad bridge was the first in the United States.

In August, 1953, the daddy of Upstate traffic jams was removed when the state opened a new cutoff for Route 5. Hitherto Routes 5 and 20 with their continuous streams of motor traffic, converged on the heart of the village, at Main Street and Central Avenue.

The new route bypasses narrow and steep Oak Hill, over which some 12,000 vehicles used to pass daily, and will split the traffic of the two great highways at a point east of the village. Thus while Silver Creek loses one of its claims to fame, its citizens will be able to walk across their principal street intersection the same day.

About that "biggest tree in the world"—it was a black walnut and it stood along the creek of that name where Main Street and Ward Avenue now join. It measured 27 feet in circumference and nine feet in diameter and its lowest limb was 70 feet above the ground.

The forest giant blew down in 1822. It was hollowed out so that it contained a room in which 39 persons could stand and 17 sit. Once it held a ladies' tea party. Then a grocer used it as an annex to his store. Travelers came to Silver Creek, in those days called Fayette, to see it, and in 1825 two local Barnums bought the great tree and started it on a tour via Erie Canal boat. At Lockport they ran out of cash and sold it to other exhibitors who took it to New York where it attracted crowds. Then the much traveled tree went overseas to London, where it was shown in a museum and advertised as "The Black Walnut from Lake Erie—Biggest in the World." Fire destroyed it and the London museum.

In 1928 Major Benjamin Bosworth Chapter of the Daughters of the American Revolution marked the site of the historic tree with a tablet mounted upon a stone taken from the town's first grist mill which was built along nearby Walnut Creek.

On August 9, 1841 the steamboat *Erie* left Buffalo for Chicago with 250 passengers, 150 of them Swiss emigrants, aboard. Off Silver Creek, varnish near the smoke stack ignited and the ship burst into flames. Two hundred and fifteen bodies were washed up on the beach of Silver Creek in that most terrible of Lake Erie tragedies. In 1838 there was another ship disaster at almost the same spot. The steamer *Washington* caught fire and 12 out of the 70 persons aboard were drowned after they leaped from the blazing vessel.

The "skew arch" stone bridge which carries the New York Central tracks over Jackson Street near the lake beach was built in 1869 and it was an engineering sensation of the time. Its designer was a French deaf mute. A "skew arch" bridge differs from the conventional type in that its outside arches are parallel to each other but not at right angles, in other words they are askew. This principle was used in the stone bridge at Silver Creek to overcome difficulties caused by the high embankments there and to add to the symmetry of the span. The "skew arch" principle is used quite often in concrete bridges today but when the old stone landmark was built at Silver Creek, it was a national oddity.

Despite village legends, removal of the keystone or central ring would not cause the bridge to collapse although it possibly might cause that particular arch to fall. But it never has in these 84 years it has been there.

Cattaraugus Creek empties into Lake Erie near Irving after coursing through the Indian reservation, which lies almost wholly in Erie County. Robert P. Galloway of Silver Creek, attorney for the Seneca Nation, informed me there are only 13 Indians living on the reservation in Chautauqua County.

Once Silver Creek was a busy port for the lake steamboats. There were heavy shipments of lumber. Ships were built and launched at Silver Creek. Between 1824 and 1844 no less than 15 craft slid down the ways there. Oliver Lee built the first wharf and a warehouse and developed the harbor. He was the leading citizen in the pioneering time and built the village's first large hotel, the present Powers. His name is on the village library. In the port's heyday there were hotels on the waterfront and black walnut trees lined Jackson Street.

The coming of the Erie Railroad to Dunkirk doomed the lake traffic. The hotels and the black walnut trees went down long ago. Now bathers splash and shout where once was a lively harbor.

Since 1864 a large grain cleaning machinery plant, the S. Howes Company, which still bears its founder's name, has been a major Silver Creek industry. Until about 20 years ago

Ward and Dickinson made lunch cars which were shipped all over the country. Among present day village industries are Forbes and Wagner, precision tool makers, and a large canning plant. The village has a considerable Italian-American population.

A mile-long shoreline lies within the village limits. There are beaches galore in that corner of Chautauqua. Along the lake west of Silver Creek is St. Columbans Seminary for foreign missionaries of the Catholic faith.

Remember big Howard Ehmke, the pitching hero of the 1929 World Series, how in the twilight of his diamond career he went on the hill for the Philadelphia Athletics in the first game of the Series and stopped the Chicago Cubs? His 13 strikeouts still stand as a World Series record. Silver Creek was Ehmke's home town. He now lives in California but old timers in his native village still talk about his pitching prowess.

South of Silver Creek a road lined with vineyards leads to Forestville, which lies in a deep valley and lives up to its name in the matter of shade trees. It was originally Walnut Falls and it is the birthplace of George Abbott, the theatrical producer, and Marvin R. Dye, now a resident of Rochester and a judge of the Court of Appeals, New York's highest tribunal.

Chapter 4

Dunkirk, Generous and Gusty

Two cities named Dunkirk, with an ocean between them, marched into the headlines during the fateful 1940s.

One was an ancient coastal city of 10,000 in the northwestern corner of France just across the strait of Dover from the English shore. The deliverance of a trapped and beaten British army from the beaches of Dunkirk in early June of 1940 is one of the most stirring stories in all history.

The other Dunkirk, a city of 18,000 on the shores of Lake Erie in Western New York state, got its name 135 years ago, because its harbor resembled that of the older port across the sea.

The story of how the younger Dunkirk gathered and sent $100,000 in emergency supplies to its stricken Old World namesake will not live in world history. Few remember it even now, but around Thanksgiving Day of 1946 thousands read the story and their hearts were touched.

It came about through an informal luncheon of some Dunkirk men in the Francis Hotel earlier that year. One of the group mentioned that he had read a story in the *Dunkirk Observer* about the sorry plight of the French Dunkirk. During the occupation, the Germans had taken away about all the people's means of livelihood, including their farming tools and stock. They had no funds to start anew.

At the luncheon table in the American city on Lake Erie was born the idea, nebulous at first, of helping the other

Dunkirk in its hour of need. An item appeared in the *Observer* and a committee was appointed, in the hope of raising at least $2,500. A mass meeting gave momentum to the drive. Every civic organization, every veteran group, every union pitched in. The whole community was aroused. Farmers of the region gave live stock. Their wives parted with their prized jellies.

So on Thanksgiving Day of 1946, the city firehouse was full of canned goods, clothing, medical and surgical supplies, farm machinery, seed, toys, kitchen utensils, besides a herd of cattle, some goats and pigs that were housed in a barn. School children brought in pencils.

That holiday brought the French ambassador, Henri Bonnet, to Dunkirk to accept the gifts before they were loaded into freight cars for their long journey. Bonnet, Charles Boyer, the film star, and Dunkirk's Mayor Walter Murray reviewed a parade of 18 trucks, laden with nearly $100,000 worth of supplies at the climax of Dunkirk's great day.

Newspapers and magazines told the world of the little city's good deed. People who had never heard of Dunkirk N. Y. were stirred by this generous second "deliverance of Dunkirk." The people of the French town sent their heartfelt thanks. But the principal gainer was Dunkirk N. Y. Its gain was in the realm of the spirit. The spirit of brotherhood which was awakened by the crusade still lingers in Dunkirk hearts.

The breezes that sweep in from spirited old Lake Erie are fresh and invigorating and perhaps they purge the Dunkirk air of the stuffiness and smugness of many of our older towns. Here is an industrial city, a melting pot, with citizens of Polish extraction making up nearly 40 per cent of its population and with a sizeable Italian-American colony. Dunkirk has had its bad times and its good times. Once it was the western terminal of the longest railroad in the world and it dreamed of metropolitan glory—only to be dwarfed by the rise of Buffalo.

From the windows of a railroad coach, the view of Dunkirk—the old part of town—is not prepossessing. Alas, the traveler does not see the shady residential streets, the parks and beaches. He should stop over and see the harbor at night—the fishing boats tied to the pier, the Mary S., the Gloria Mae, the Eleanor D., and the rest, see the nets drying on the racks at the commercial fish houses—the lights glistening on the water, the lights of the pleasure craft and of the great throbbing power generating station on the point—the people in the city park along the shore, young lovers and older people who speak with Old World accents. That is Dunkirk harbor at night, one of the most fascinating places in the Southern Tier.

* * *

Dunkirk's first settler was Solomon Chadwick in 1809 and its first name was Chadwick's Bay. There was only a tiny settlement until 1818 when a group of speculators, headed by De Witt Clinton, father of the Erie Canal and then governor of New York, bought 1,000 acres fronting "the best natural harbor on Lake Erie" and laid out a village site.

The land agent for the enterprise was Daniel G. Garnsey and for a time the settlement was known as Garnsey's Bay. It was another of the proprietors, Elisha Jenkins, who gave the place its present name. He had been in the shipping business in France and was struck by the resemblance between the harbor on Lake Erie and the one at Dunkirk on the North Sea.

The Clinton group built a wharf, a warehouse and other buildings. In 1820 a lighthouse was erected at Point Gratiot, the rugged headland on the lake which was named after an army officer and is now a municipal park.

In 1825 the proprietors sold half their interest to Walter Smith, aggressive 25-year-old merchant of Fredonia. He played a considerable role in the early development of Dunkirk. Smith built roads, established stage lines, boosted lake shipping and was one of the early promoters of the New York and Erie Railroad.

The bold plan to link the Hudson with Lake Erie by the longest railroad in the world took shape in the early 1830s. It grew from the alarm of the southern counties because of their isolation after the completion of the Erie Canal and of their determination to have a commercial outlet. The railroad was chartered in 1832 but work did not commence until 1835—at the eastern terminal, Piermont on the Hudson. It was 16 years before it reached Lake Erie.

After Dunkirk, a lake port midway between Buffalo and Erie, was picked as the western terminal of the new trunk line, the village went mad with speculation on corner lots and building sites. A big hotel was begun. Later on it became the Loder House, in honor of Ben Loder, president of the Erie. Land was given for a depot. Walter Smith planted hickory trees on Point Gratiot and Dunkirk dreamed of becoming a metropolis.

The choice of Dunkirk as the railroad terminal dashed the hopes of the New York City men who had gambled on Van Buren, on the lake to the southwest, and had laid out a future city there. Van Buren Point is a pleasant summer colony today and nothing more.

Dunkirk's dream of glory was rudely interrupted by the panic of 1837. The Erie was at a standstill. There were financial barriers to hurdle as well as the formidable hills. Walter Smith's financial structure tottered. The big hotel stood, unfinished, with spiders and bats its only guests. Cows roamed the streets.

The hard times passed. The pace of railroad building quickened. The Erie inched westward. Dunkirk stirred again. The Loder House was finished and a lakeside village, gay with flags and bunting, welcomed the first Erie train which on May 15, 1851, steamed under a great arch into the depot near the lake. In the harbor the USS Michigan lay at anchor, surrounded by decorated lake craft of all sizes.

The ship guns boomed out the Presidential salute, for President Millard Fillmore was on that historic special train, along with Secretary of State Daniel Webster and most of the other cabinet members. Webster rode across the state in a rocking chair lashed to a flat car. The statesman wanted to view the scenery.

In Dunkirk, 15,000 people were served a barbecue on a single table 300 feet long, in a pavilion which stretched along Railroad Avenue from Deer Street to Lion Street. Then came feasting and oratory at the Loder House.

It was an epochal event. The Hudson and the Great Lakes were linked by 483 miles of rails. It had taken 16 years and 23 million dollars but at last the Southern Tier had its railroad to compete with the Clinton Ditch. And for Dunkirk, the western terminal of that railroad, with its new car shops and fine lake harbor, the future had rainbow hues.

But almost at once the Erie promoters saw that they had erred in their choice of terminals. They should have chosen Buffalo, not Dunkirk, and Jersey City, not Piermont. In time those points became the terminals. Only a year after the completion of the line from Piermont to Dunkirk, a branch was built from Hornellsville to Buffalo and it diverted a lot of traffic from the western end.

In 1869 the Erie abandoned its Dunkirk shops but Horatio Brooks, who had been a division superintendent of the railroad, leased them and organized the Brooks Locomotive Works. That became the present plant of the American Locomotive Company. Locomotives were made in Dunkirk until 1928.

Dunkirk's importance as a lake port waned with the coming of the railroads. For a long time her wharves were busy places. First steamboat to dock at Dunkirk and the first on the lakes was the *Walk in the Water,* which arrived in 1818 when there were only 20 buildings in the village.

Lake traffic continued heavy through the 1840s. A boat would leave Buffalo at 9 P.M., discharge and take on passengers and freight at Silver Creek, Dunkirk and Barcelona and reach Erie, Pa., at dawn. Freight boats made Dunkirk a regular port of call until after the Civil War.

There are dangerous reefs along the picturesque lake coast and in 1893 the propeller ship, the *Dean Richmond,* foundered off Van Buren Point, its wreckage was strewn along the beach and 18 lives were lost.

Nowadays an occasional freighter docks at Dunkirk with a load of sand. Its excellent harbor is a refuge and a playground for pleasure craft. And the commercial fishing fleet still goes out from Dunkirk pier. You will find from eight to 10 fishing boats tied up there at night.

Commercial fishing goes back to 1851 when Irish-born James Malony equipped a row boat with gill nets and made his own nets and rig. Then came the Johnson brothers from Fort Erie, Ont., with home-made nets and a 26 foot sailing skiff. They used flat stones to weigh down their nets.

At its peak the fishing industry employed 200 men. In the 1880s the main catch was ciscoes. In the 1890s Lake Erie sturgeon were shipped to faraway markets and Van Buren

Bay was called Sturgeon Bay. In 1898 the first steam tugs appeared. Old newspaper files tell of fabulous catches and of dramatic rescues of fishermen, trapped in the ice.

Commercial fishing is not what it used to be. But what is? The main catch now is bluepike and whitefish, sold to the local fish companies.

Dunkirk's principal industries are Allegheny Ludlom Steel, American Locomotive, which makes pipe, power plant equipment and other things, but no locomotives, and Van Raalte, producers of women's lingerie and gloves. None of these is locally owned. Other Dunkirk plants produce such items as radiators, boilers, tools and dies, airplane parts, brass valves, engine rods. The grape belt city also has a jam and jelly plant and a sizeable brewery. All of which adds up to considerable industrial diversity.

All is not smoking chimneys and work in this lakeside town. There are three miles of shoreline within the city limits and several handy bathing beaches. And there is the County Fair every Fall in Dunkirk.

Along Central Avenue, not far from downtown, is a spacious, comfortable white house with a famous occupant. But he does not spend much time there. Daniel A. Reed, 75-year-old chairman of the House Ways and Means Committee, dean of the Congress with his 35 years of service, is pretty busy in Washington most of the time.

His one-man battle for elimination of the corporation excess profit tax, in defiance of President Eisenhower's stand, made headline news in 1953. Dan Reed, former Cornell football star and coach, stands up and fights for what he thinks is right. Dunkirk people believe in him and support him to the hilt.

The Dunkirk region was the scene of a naval engagement of the War of 1812 and the fearless ride of a "Pauline Revere."

A handful of militia was stationed at the home of the widow Cole where the Canadaway Creek pours into Lake Erie. A British cruiser came off the lake to chase a salt boat in the creek. The militia drove off a boarding party from the British ship with their muskets and a swivel cannon hidden in the crotch of a big elm tree. The Redcoats withdrew with a loss of 10 killed and wounded of their crew of 13. There were no American casualties.

When the shooting began, the widow Cole saddled a horse and rode to Fredonia, sounding the alarm and rallying more men to the mouth of the creek. On her return trip she carried food and drink to the defenders. It was hardly a major battle but it is said to have been the first naval engagement of the war.

In 1834 a young carpenter and joiner came to Dunkirk. He helped build some of the older houses in the town. His name was Erastus Dow Palmer and he won renown as a sculptor in marble. His "White Captive" is one of the treasures of the Metropolitan Museum of Art in New York.

Mary Ellen Lease was born in Dunkirk but she won her fame, such as it was, on the plains of Kansas. A leader of the Populist movement in the 1890s, an Amazonian figure with a golden voice, she once implored her fellow Kansans to raise more hell and less corn.

Long ago somebody—nobody seems to know who—gave Dunkirk streets the names of animals, birds and fish. There are names like Antelope, Armadillo, Dove, Eagle, Lynx, Pike, Plover, Robin, Swan and Zebra. There also are such obscure names as Genet, Jerboa, Ocelot and Zorilla. That last one is not gorilla misspelled. The zorilla, according to the dictionary, is a skunk-like animal found in South Africa.

The slogan of this interesting city which basks in the breezes of Lake Erie might well be: "Dunkirk is different."

Chapter 5

Fredonia—Traditions, Tourists and Teachers

Fredonia and Dunkirk have a common street—Central Avenue. Only a sign at the boundary line tells the visitor where Dunkirk leaves off and Fredonia begins.

But Fredonia and Dunkirk, despite their proximity, are no more alike than John L. Lewis and Emily Post. It's not a matter of size either, although Dunkirk, a city of 18,000, is more than twice as large as Fredonia, a village of 7,000.

Dunkirk is overalls and oilskins. Fredonia is lavender and old lace. Industrial Dunkirk is impulsive, breezy like the lake on its border and is of the living, breathing present. Residential Fredonia is steeped in tradition and history. Fredonia is the place of the twin commons with the historical markers, the tourists and the teachers' college, the authors and the big names and the mansions haunted by the shades of the illustrious dead.

Few villages of its size can boast as many "firsts" as Fredonia. The boulders and the markers tell you that here was the first natural gas well in the United States, the first chapter of the Women's Christian Temperance Union, the first unit of the National Grange.

Chauncey M. Depew, who for so long represented the New York Central in the United States Senate, once called Fredonia the most beautiful village in America. But the urbane banquet orator might have said the same thing in 50 other villages in his long career.

Twilight at Chautauqua—Palestine Park and Miller Bell Tower

Chautauqua Institution's Hall of Philosophy

Fredonia unquestionably is one of the most attractive communities in the Southern Tier, with its canopy of trees, its broad streets, its parks, its old homes, and its air of distinction. No factory smoke stains the historic buildings. Its industries, evidence of its location in the fruit and farm belt along Lake Erie, are a plant which processes fruit juices and jellies, two canneries and three seed companies.

Fredonia, which is in the town of Pomfret, was settled in 1803 by three Pennsylvanians and was first known as Canadaway after the creek of that name. In 1806 Hezekiah Barker bought out the Pennsylvanians and built a log tavern. He was one of the pillars of the settlement. In 1825 he gave the twin Barker Commons in the heart of the village, the first public park in Chautauqua County. In the early days justices of the peace, under the terms of a village law, sentenced each convicted drunk to pull a stump in the park and in that way it was soon cleared. Old residents recall when there was a fence around the commons to which horses were tied.

Here's another tale of the pioneers. One Summer wild pigeons flew over the lakeside from their roosts in Pennsylvania and Canada in such numbers that the pioneers batted them down with poles, killing 4,000 in one day. Many a family feasted on pigeon pie. 'Tis said that when the bird horde took off, the roar of the wings was like rolling thunder and in steady flight it was like the rush of a great wind.

Fredonia had high hopes of being named the shire town when Chautauqua County was formed in 1808 and land was cleared on West Hill for the county buildings, but Mayville, the seat of the land office, took the prize.

There's another common on West Hill and a boulder honoring the memory of Judge Jacob Houghton and his son, Douglas, an eminent naturalist who is credited with discovering the first iron ore in Minnesota. Judge Houghton, one of the leading pioneers, is supposed to have first suggested the name, Fredonia, an Indian word meaning "free woman," and once proposed as the name of these United States.

William A. Hart, a Fredonia gunsmith, was a persistent cuss. He knew there was natural gas on his land in the bed of Canadaway Creek. He broke and lost a drill in his first attempt at drilling. Hart hammered out his own tools and sunk a second well, but the flow was meager. The third time, and near the scene of the two previous failures, he struck a good volume of gas at 70 feet. That was in 1821 and it was the first natural gas well in the United States.

Hart began to market the gas which was carried in lead pipes to the business places of the village. His first customer was a tavern keeper on the stage coach route opposite the well. Soon the village street lamps were burning gas. Travelers came to marvel at the brilliantly illuminated village.

A most distinguished visitor came to Fredonia in 1825. He was the aging Marquis de Lafayette, on his grand tour of the country he had befriended in its revolution when he was young. It was 2 o'clock in the morning when his stage coach arrived from Westfield but the crowd was still waiting. A cannon salute and a parade of soldiers greeted the famous Frenchman and his retinue. There was a banquet in the tavern under the gas lights. The visitors were enchanted with "the gas that came from the ground."

Lafayette's secretary wrote in his journal: "I shall never forget the magical effect produced at Fredonia. Our eyes were dazzled by the glare of a thousand lights, suspended to the houses and trees that surrounded us."

From a platform in the park Lafayette and other dignitaries greeted the villagers who lined up to meet the hero of the Revolution. The wife of the Episcopal rector had loaned her parlor carpet for that platform and it was worn thin by tramping feet. One village woman who owned a handsome shawl passed it from back to back. After the reception the Marquis remarked on the elegance of Fredonia's women. He said he had never seen so many handsome shawls.

During the long wait for Lafayette, a candle in a second story window of the elegant brick home of General Barker, now the village public library, built in 1818, burned too low. The charred window sill is still there, after 128 years.

And in the circle of the village seal is a standard with five flaming gas lights. Also there is a boulder with a tablet on it, beside the bridge on Fredonia's Main Street, to mark the site of the first gas well in America.

Teachers have been trained in Fredonia for 85 years. The present State Teachers College, it was Fredonia Normal until 1942, grew out of the old Fredonia Academy, which was built by funds raised by the people and which began life in 1826 with three teachers.

That old Academy in its time was the center of light and learning in the region and numbered among its students a future governor, Reuben E. Fenton; a future Civil War general, George A. Stoneman, and a future Naval hero of the Civil War, William B. Cushing. Cushing, the scion of Fredonia pioneers, was admitted to the Naval Academy at Annapolis at the age of 14 and he was only 22 when he destroyed the Confederate ironclad, *Albemarle,* in a North Carolina harbor with his own hands. Cushing dived under the ship and placed the charge that blew it up.

In 1866 Willard McKinstry, editor of the *Fredonia Censor,* noticed among the legal advertising an act of the state legislature providing for four more state normal schools. McKinstry started a movement to get one of those schools for Fredonia. Both the governor, Reuben E. Fenton, and the state superintendent of public instruction, Victor Rice, were Chautauqua men and that helped in Albany. At a conference of Fredonians called by McKinstry, the village pledged $100,000 and won the Normal School. The school opened in February of 1868 on the Temple Street site it has since occupied. The old Academy was used until a new building was completed that Fall.

Flames swept that building on the night of December 14, 1900 with tragic loss of life. The blaze, starting in the basement, spread rapidly. All the students in the south wing dormitory escaped but in the north wing, the girls who ran to the fire escape found the way to safety barred by a netted screen so tight it could not be removed. Some stepped out windows and crept along an ice-coated ledge. Seven young women students and the janitor perished. The girls were buried in a common grave.

The sprawling structure, still on the campus and known to so many hundreds of graduates as "Old Main," replaced the fire-ravaged building. Now a new administration building and dormitories are being built on a new site out Central Avenue. The State Teachers College has an enrollment of about 800. It is not only an economic asset to Fredonia but it gives the village a college town atmosphere and adds to the cultural tone the community has always had.

Diagonally across from "Old Main" at Central Avenue and Temple Street a pillared mansion stands on an eminence. It's a funeral home now but once a drawling humorist, a onetime river boat pilot, wearing a scraggy white mustache and a white suit, used to visit his niece's husband who owned that mansion.

The visitor was Samuel Langhorne Clemens, better known under his writing name of Mark Twain, and the host was Charles L. Webster. The two men joined in publishing General Grant's memoirs, which Grant completed almost with his dying breath. Webster wrote a biography of Pope Leo XIII which pleased the pontiff so much he made the Fredonian a knight of the Church.

In later years in that same old house, a daughter of Webster and a grandniece of Mark Twain, Jean Webster (Mrs. Glenn Ford McKinney) wrote *When Patty Went to College* and other tales for girls. Her most famous opus was *Daddy Longlegs,* which she made into a play and which became a silent movie in which Mary Pickford starred.

Still living on Fredonia's East Main Street, an old lady now, is Grace S. Richmond, author of the once popular *Red Pepper Burns* books. Richard T. Ely, who became an eminent educator and political economist, was born and raised in Fredonia.

Mary E. ("Pants") Walker, celebrated in her time as an eccentric feminist and advocate of mannish dress for women, once resided in Fredonia in a house on East Main Street. The "big names" list seems endless.

Around Barker Commons are grouped the city hall, the fire hall, the postoffice and four churches. In one of those houses of worship, the Baptist church with its dignified clock tower, a determined band of 208 women met and organized on December 15, 1873 what is claimed to be the first unit of the Women's Christian Temperance Union. In the park across the way is a memorial to the leader of that crusade, Mrs. Esther McNeil. In each common is a drinking fountain with the name, Mark, on it. The fountains have nothing to do with Mark Twain. Charles L. Mark, a village business man, provided them.

Near the Common also is a building that is a sort of memorial to a departed form of transportation, the electric trolley. Now buses are stored in the former car barn of the electric line which began service between Fredonia and Dunkirk in 1890. It supplanted the first horse car line in the county, established in 1866.

In 1868 O. H. Kelley, the youthful Minnesota man who conceived the idea of banding the farmers of the nation together into the National Grange or Patrons of Husbandry, came East to organize Grange units. He tried in vain in Harrisburg, Pa., and in Penn Yan, N. Y. In Fredonia he had better success. Nine men organized in the grape belt village the first subordinate Grange in America. Grange Hall on Main Street has a sign on it which reads: "Grange No. I." A Fredonian, Sherman J. Lowell, served as state and national master of the Grange.

So many Fredonia enterprises have their roots deep in the past. The village newspaper, the *Censor,* goes back to 1821. Obeying his own advice to "Go West, young man," young Horace Greeley, a tramp printer in 1830, got as far West as Fredonia and for a time set type in the *Censor* office.

A short-lived early industry was the manufacture of silk. But the housing of the silk worms in the Winter raised a problem and the climate of the Southern Tier was not conducive to the raising of mulberry trees.

Business enterprises which once carried the name of Fredonia all over the land were the patent medicine house established by Dr. Milton M. Fenner and the Risley Seed Gardens whose wagons traveled the roads of many states.

Watches once were manufactured in Fredonia. One of the local watchmakers, Frank Howard, got the idea of sending a watch to railroad station agents throughout the country on consignment. If the agent sold the watch, he got a commission and could order more. Otherwise he could return the timepiece.

One of the Howard watches fell into the hands of an agent

in a little station in Illinois. His name was Sears and he disposed of the first watch so easily he sent back for more. He figured that if watches could be sold by mail, so could hundreds of other articles. He interested a man named Roebuck in his mail order scheme and—you know the rest of the story.

But I hardly think even Fredonia, home of so many firsts, can claim to be the actual birthplace of Sears, Roebuck.

Chapter 6

Vineyard Villages—Brocton, Westfield, Ripley

In 1818 Elijah Fay, a Yankee and a deacon of the Baptist church, planted the first grape vines in New York State west of the Hudson. Seven years before, he had come to the town of Portland and after clearing his land along Lake Erie, found it suitable for the growing of apples and pears.

He began experimenting with grapes and in 1830 he made five gallons of wine from the Isabella and Catawba vines he had planted. That was the start of Chautauqua County's great vineyard industry.

Deacon Fay and the other settlers who planted vineyards thought of grapes only in terms of wine and they operated wineries.

They would be amazed to learn that today very little of the enormous crop of the Chautauqua vineyards, by far the largest in the state, goes into wine—that their old stamping ground is the Grape Juice Country.

That is because of the fanatical prohibition beliefs of two New Jersey dentists, father and son, who founded what became the largest grape juice company in the world and made the village of Westfield the Grape Juice capital.

That industry was born in the Vineland N. J. kitchen of Dr. Thomas B. Welch's home. Welch had been a preacher and a physician before he became a dentist. He was an inveterate foe of the demon rum and when his church made him its communion steward, he resolved to find a substitute for wine.

For months in 1869 he and his 17-year-old son, Charles, littered Mrs. Welch's kitchen with their pots and funnels and bottles before they finally succeeded in getting "unfermented wine" from Concord grapes.

The process was simple. First they cooked the grapes on the kitchen stove for a few minutes. Then they squeezed out the juice through cloth bags. Next they filtered it and poured the world's first processed fruit juice into twelve quart bottles on the kitchen table.

Keeping it from fermenting was the crux of their problem. After stoppering the bottles with cork and wax, they lowered them into boiling water. They were following the theory of the French scientist, Louis Pasteur, that heat kills the yeast organisms which cause fermentation. Welch's juice did not ferment. Word of his success spread and he began filling orders for other congregations who wanted no alcohol at their communion tables.

In 1873 Doctor Welch sold his modest juice business to a neighbor. Two years later young Charles, who also had become a dentist, bought it back. The rest of his 51 years were to be devoted to the Welch Grape Juice Company and to the cause of prohibition.

Charles Welch was not content with a little business. He began to advertise and to expand. He ran a booth at the Chicago World's Fair in 1893 where he sold iced grape juice at five cents a glass. The drink was vastly popular and soon the Welch business in Vineland was taxing the capacity of its plant and the supply of Concord grapes in the region.

Welch sought a new location. After two years in Watkins Glen in the Finger Lakes country, he came to Westfield in 1896. He built his first plant on North Portage Street the next year. That building now is the print shop of the giant Welch company.

Ever since Deacon Fay's time there had been vineyards and wineries on the sunny shores of Lake Erie. Welch began buying all the grapes the farmers could produce and he urged them to plant more. Before long nearly the whole yield of the Chautauqua region was going into Welch grape juice.

Welch built a big new plant and a big new office building in Westfield. He started a plant in nearby Brocton. He advertised widely, always preaching prohibition in his ads. One read: "The lips that touch Welch's are all that touch mine."

The business which had begun in a Jersey kitchen flourished, aided by Secretary of State William Jennings Bryan's serving of grape juice at state dinners and by Secretary of the Navy Daniels' outlawing liquor on warships.

Welch ran for governor of New York on the Prohibition ticket in 1916. That was good advertising, too, but Welch ran because of his deep convictions. He was no charlatan.

Welch died in 1926—while prohibition was still in flower. After his death a banking syndicate ran the business until its purchase in 1945 by Jacob M. Kaplan, a self-made New Yorker.

Kaplan introduced many innovations. He began by offering growers a flat price guaranty for their crop. He added new lines, concentrates and jellies. And now for the first time in its history, Welch's is making wine, not on a large scale yet, in its Brocton plant.

Besides the plants in Westfield, Brocton and in nearby North East, Pa., there are two in Michigan, one in Arkansas and one in the State of Washington.

In 1952 a significant, almost revolutionary step in industry was taken when the Welch Company and the National Grape Co-operative Association, made up of 4,000 growers in seven states, signed a contract whereby the growers eventually will own the whole industry. Each year a percentage of sales is credited to the co-op until the total purchase price, fifteen millions, is paid off.

The modern manufacture of grape juice follows basically the pattern set in the Welch kitchen in 1869. After the grapes are harvested—and the harvest is a stupendous thing every Fall in the Chautauqua belt—they are trucked in crates to the plants where they are washed and stemmed.

Then they go to the cooking rooms and into stainless steel tanks. The next step is the forming of the juice into a huge "cheese," composed of layers of grapes folded into cotton blankets, three tons of hot grapes on a steel cart. The cart is rolled under a hydraulic plunger which applies 150 tons of pressure to the mass for an hour. Cascades of deep purple juice pour out of the sides of the "cheese." Pipes carry the juice off to be pasteurized, tested and sent on to the bottling line.

* * *

The lakeside grape belt is dotted with pleasant communities, each with its bits of history, lore and legend. One of those villages is Brocton (population 1,380) in the town of Portland. Until some 30 years ago the village was the scene of an annual grape festival. Now the event, with the traditional parade, floats and coronation, is held in North East, just over the Pennsylvania line. Near Brocton is a railroad station named Concord, after the grape that gave the region fame.

A lakeside farm near Brocton once was the site of one of the most fantastic colonies in America. In 1867 Thomas

Lake Harris, a onetime New York City pastor, a traveling lecturer and a poet, who composed his verse while in a trance, a mystic and a prophet who received "revelations" from on high, bought 2,000 acres in Chautauqua County. Earlier he had founded a small colony, the Brotherhood of the New Life, in Dutchess County.

He taught humility, the divinity of labor—by other hands than his—and the divinity of Thomas Lake Harris. He was an impressive figure of a man in his fine clothes and his flowing beard and he had a magnetic way with him.

Otherwise he would never have so bewitched Lawrence Oliphant, whom he had met in London, that the young English member of parliament left a promising political and social career to become a virtual slave of the bearded prophet. His mother, Lady Oliphant, widow of a former attorney general of South Africa, also came under the Harris spell and accompanied her son to the colony along Lake Erie which had been bought with Oliphant money.

For 14 years the former English MP and his titled mother were dominated by the tyrannical lord of the lakeside colony which he renamed the Use. They were forced to do the most menial tasks. Harris' word was law. His mastery over them seems inexplicable. But Harris also at various times numbered among his converts Japanese dignitaries, Indian princes and American socialites.

The prophet was a practical man. His subjects raised large crops of hay and grapes. He built a restaurant at the railroad station where wine and fruit were sold to travelers. Lawrence Oliphant hawked those wares on the trains.

At last the Oliphants rebelled. Their erstwhile lord and master knew then the jig was up and Thomas Lake Harris took himself, his tall silk hat and his magnetic manner, to California. Oliphant went to the courts to gain possession of the Brocton property. He never returned to the scene of his long degradation.

Brocton is the birthplace of George M. Pullman, who made millions out of the sleeping car he invented. His father, Lewis, patented a method of moving buildings while the family lived in Brocton, before moving to Albion in 1844.

A playground of the Grape Juice Belt is the 240-acre Lake Erie State Park along Route 5, north of Brocton, with its bathing beaches and wide open spaces.

* * *

An Old World air invests the little port with the old Spanish name of Barcelona, where Route 17 ends at Lake Erie's edge, with its old stone lighthouse, the commercial fishing boats in the cove, the nets on the racks, the quaint old inn and the wheeling gulls.

It was at Barcelona that the Frenchmen under Celoron landed in 1749 before they marched over the Portage Road.

Barcelona's harbor attracted land speculators who laid out a village and dreamed of a great port there. They built a steamboat which they called the William Peacock, after the Mayville land agent, in 1831. For a score of years the lake boats on the Buffalo-Erie run stopped at Barcelona.

In 1828 the government built the stone lighthouse on the hill. It was the first lighthouse lighted by gas in the world. When gas was discovered three quarters of a mile away in 1831, it was piped to the lighthouse through a wooden main. The gas-fed beacon shone out on the lake for many years. Now the lighthouse and the adjoining keeper's residence is a private home.

Barcelona has been a fishing port for many years. The scene is the same as in Dunkirk harbor, only more sylvan. There are the fishing boats, two to eight of them tied to the pier, the nets drying on the racks, the fish houses. Each diesel-powered boat, manned by a captain and four deckhands, spreads its nylon gill net from five to eight miles out in the lake. Young John Monroe is the third generation of his family among the Barcelona commercial fishermen.

White fish is the principal catch. Most of the yield of the Barcelona fishing fleet is shipped to New York. Some is sold right in the port. The old inn is famous for its fish dinners.

Barcelona is tiny but different.

* * *

Westfield is known in far places at the home of the Welch Grape Juice Company. It is familiar to thousands of tourists as the junction of Route 20, the road to Cleveland and the West, and Route 17, the road to Chautauqua Lake. On many of Westfield's fine old homes you see the sign "Tourists and Antiques."

This attractive village of 3,600 people has a high place in regional history. Through the site of Westfield ran the trail known to the Indians and to Celoron's French soldiers and the Portage Road the French built in 1753. Westfield's Portage Street and Route 17 follow pretty much the old pre-revolutionary trail.

It was in Westfield that Colonel James McMahan made the first permanent settlement in Chautauqua County in 1802. Westfield was the first postoffice in the county.

It is fitting that at Westfield's busy and historic crossroads, the treasures of the past should be displayed, in a gracious and distinctive old white house, which is the headquarters and museum of the Chautauqua County Historical Society.

The landmark was built in 1818–1820 by James McClurg, a Scottish-Irish trader from Pittsburgh, in front of his earlier log cabin-trading post. It is in the style of a Scottish manor house and sets well back from the principal street, facing the green plot which was long ago given the town for a common.

In 1836–38 William H. Seward occupied the house and used its "octagon room" as his office while he was agent for the Holland Land Company in a time of turmoil.

Westfield people speak of the place as "the Moore house," because of the long residence there of Dr. William J. Moore, a grandson of James McClurg. Doctor Moore bequeathed the house to the village which in 1950 leased it to the Chautauqua Historical Society for 75 years. The village already had Eason Hall as a meeting place, a gift of one of the numerous pioneer families.

The society's relics were brought from Mayville and the History Center, with its high ceilinged rooms, its winding staircases, its many fireplaces, was restored in the proper period. The collection has been augmented by gifts since the society acquired the museum until today it is one of the finest regional historical exhibits in the state. And its curator, Orry Heath, is a well informed guide.

The visitor sees at the History Center the hand-wrought, 500 pound safe, the high bookkeeper's desk and account books of land agents Seward and his successor, George W. Patterson, one of Westfield's first citizens. Also in the "octagon room" that was their office is the small safe saved from the farmers who raided the land office at Mayville in the "land war" of 1835. Also on display are Governor Fenton's tall silk hat and his desk and the finery his wife wore abroad.

There is parched corn, 400 years old and dug up from the site of an Indian village, and pottery, made by a prehistoric people, which was excavated recently in the Westfield area and the shattered bits carefully pieced together.

There are relics of the pioneers—bear traps, horn-handled

deer knives, broad axes, bark peelers, a "bull" plow, mortars and pestles, winnowers and flails. Of interest to anglers are oldtime "muskie" spears, a torch basket for lake fishermen's boats, hand-made spinners of copper, brass and silver. Ice-cutting tools tell of oldtime harvests on Chautauqua Lake.

There is furniture to gladden the heart of the lovers of antiques, pewter 250 years old, paintings of the pioneers and of regional scenes, a conch horn which called in the hands from the fields, a French bayonet believed to have belonged to one of Celoron's men.

In the History Center also is a framed copy of the letter Abraham Lincoln wrote in 1860 to an 11-year-old Westfield girl. It was in answer to one Grace Bedell wrote to the Republican nominee for President, suggesting that "he would look a lot better if he wore whiskers" and promising to get her brothers to vote for him if he would grow a beard. Lincoln indicated that he didn't think a beard would help his appearance. But when he came through Westfield in 1861 on his way to Washington for the inauguration and asked to speak to Grace Bedell, he was wearing a beard.

In the heart of Westfield a long viaduct carries Route 20 over a ravine. That ravine is a continuation of the spectacular Chautauqua Gorge, which reaches its zenith at "the Hog's Back," along Route 17 on the road to Mayville. There the banks of the steep canyon are 2,000 feet above sea level as Chautauqua Creek cleaves through the summit of the "great divide," the water shed, in its rapid descent to join Lake Erie.

* * *

Ripley, in the extreme southwestern corner of the fruit belt, is only a couple of miles from the Pennsylvania state line. Before New York State tightened its laws against hasty

Lake Erie's Rugged Shore near Dunkirk

"Three Sisters" at Rock City near Olean

marriages, it was a Gretna Green. Rival justices of the peace vied for the marriage business. Some had signs in front of their homes and they were open "to the trade" day and night.

Ripley also is the birthplace of Benjamin F. Goodrich, the rubber tycoon. But he didn't stay long in the village. Ripley also was the home of the late Joseph A. McGinnies, a power in state politics as the Old Guard GOP leader of the Assembly.

Its most prominent citizen during the first 40 years of this century was Charles M. Hamilton, successively member of Assembly, state senator and Congressman. He once was Republican whip of the House. He was a genial sportsman, a popular politician, who had made a fortune in Western oil lands.

He married Bertha Lamberton, daughter of a Franklin, Pa., banker. In 1924 the Hamiltons built on Ripley's West Main Street a mansion that was the showplace of the village, with its gold-painted great hall, its black Italian marble staircase, its paneled rooms, its spacious landscaped grounds and formal gardens.

The childless couple loved all dumb animals, especially dogs. "Charley" Hamilton bred hunting dogs and entered them in field trials and shows all over the country. His kennel had a sun room in it.

Hamilton died in 1942. His widow passed on two years later. Under her will, the $750,000 estate, including the mansion, was left "for the aid and comfort of dumb animals under the Hamilton Foundation for Dumb Animals." The fund was to be administered by a board of trustees, one of whom was Supreme Court Justice Alonzo G. Hinkley of Buffalo.

Relatives waged a long fight in the courts to break the

unusual will. In 1949 they lost in the highest state court and the fund was made available. The trustees faced a knotty problem. How were the terms of the will to be carried out? Was the finest house in Ripley to be converted into a big free dog and cat hospital and pound, over the protests of the veterinarians of the region?

Finally the trustees found a way to use the estate for dumb animals without opening a free pound or violating the spirit of the Hamilton will.

So today there is on the grounds of the former Hamilton estate a $45,000 building, the Hamilton Hospital for Animals, a veterinary diagnostic laboratory, with a scientific program for control of diseases in animals and serving four Western New York counties. Its director is the able Dr. W. M. Evans, for 17 years director of a similar laboratory at Cornell University.

The most important part of the program, which is carried on in co-operation with the State Department of Agriculture, is in the control of brucellosis in cattle. This disease, similar to undulant fever in humans, is the bane of the dairy farmer. Infected animals must be destroyed. Since the clinic was opened in 1950, Doctor Evans and his aides have examined 39,000 blood samples from Western New York dairy herds.

Important work also is being carried on in control of poultry diseases. The 1951 report shows tests made also for diseases in pigs, dogs, sheep, goats, a rabbit and a mouse. The hospital also serves as an emergency pound for the Town of Ripley but it houses few animals and few stay there long. The mansion is not an animal hospital. It houses the public library under an arrangement between the trustees of the fund and the village, as well as living quarters for the hospital staff.

On taking over, Doctor Evans stated the policy of the lab

would be to "use the available funds . . . to provide the greatest services, not only to animals but also to the public." That is being done—with a $750,000 legacy under one of the strangest wills ever filed in Chautauqua County.

Chapter 7

Lily Dale, "Voices from Beyond"

In the rolling hills, six miles south of Fredonia and close to Route 60, lie four pretty lakes. Water lilies lift their graceful heads above the waters and the green woods line their shores.

Three of them have the old Indian name of Cassadaga which means "the lake under the rocks." They are the Lower, Middle and Upper Cassadaga Lakes. Their smaller, obscure sister is plain Mud Lake. The Indians loved that land of lakes well for they left many evidences of their occupation in those hills.

At the foot of the Lower Lake is the rural village of Cassadaga. The Upper and Middle Lakes are so connected that they surround a heavily-wooded island. On that island is a community that is not an ordinary Summer resort nor is it an ordinary Chautauqua County village.

It has a Summer resort air. There are comfortable wooden cottages along tree-lined streets, a few business places and a huge wooden auditorium. There is a famous name on the arch above the gates to this little city and on a bulletin board nailed to a giant tree, you read such signs as:

"Trumpet seance, trance clairvoyance, automatic writing, spiritual healing, readings and circles, healing classes, psychic and astrologist."

This is Lily Dale Assembly, and the brochure handed you at the gate tells you it is "the world center of Spiritualism."

For seventy-four Summers, the faithful have been gathering beside the lakes in the hills at this shrine of their faith. They are earnest people and they believe that the "rappings" two little girls heard and answered in a cottage in Wayne County in 1848 solved the riddle of the ages and they are comforted in the belief that they can communicate with departed loved ones.

The cottage that is the birthplace of their mighty church is in Lily Dale's "Forest Temple," where outdoor services are held. The humble home in which Margaret and Katy Fox first heard the mysterious voices from beyond the grave was moved in 1916 from Hydesville near Newark to the Cassadaga Lakes.

The dilapidated old house was restored in its new site. Today there is a plaque in its yard and inside, according to the assembly program, "raps are still heard with medium Flo Cottrell of Holland, N. Y. demonstrating the same phenomena that distinguished the Fox sisters."

Long before the Spiritualists came to "the Island," it was a popular picnic spot. In September of 1852 the Lower Lake was the scene of tragedy. Seven young women and a boatman were drowned when a scow carrying 30 young people to the picnic ground upset. A steamboat once plowed the calm waters of the Cassadaga Lakes.

The Spiritualists began holding picnics in Alden's grove on "the Island" in the early 1870's. Their first camp meeting was held there in 1877 and two years later the assembly was founded and dedicated to "free thought, free speech and free investigation." Before its name was changed to Lily Dale in the early 1900s, the colony was "The City of Light."

Lily Dale, owned by a membership corporation, comprises about 180 acres, all generously forested, and 205 homes. The official summer season extends from June 27 to September 6 but a number of colonists live at Lily Dale the year around. There are two hotels, and the usual number of stores and shops you find in a Summer colony.

The central meeting place is the big wooden Auditorium, where the lectures, spirit greetings, concerts and seances are held. A dance in the Auditorium is a feature of the opening day program. Lily Dale has its traditions, just as its famous neighbor assembly on Chautauqua Lake does.

The Lily Dale program is a rather elaborate one. On it appear as lecturers the leaders of the church. Beside the Auditorium gatherings, there are "thought exchanges" in the Assembly Hall; outdoor meetings in the Forest Temple and at the "stump" in the Leolyn Woods. And there are the hundreds of private seances, readings and circles in the homes of the many mediums on the grounds. The mediums flock there in the Summer from all over the land.

The general offices of the Lily Dale Association are in the Marion Skidmore Library, a modern building standing out among its older wooden neighbors. The president of the association is William A. Johnson, a vigorous, sandy-haired, former Buffalo tax attorney in his sixties, who lives the year around on the assembly grounds.

President Johnson speaks with patent sincerity and with a persuasive eloquence of the ideals of his faith. He deplores trends toward "commercialization." He spoke feelingly of Lily Dale and its people. "We live close to nature in this tranquil place," he said. "And we live long. One man who has been coming here for 50 years is 104 years old. Another is 95. Generations of the same family come year after year to Lily Dale."

They come from all over the country. Twenty-nine states were represented in the license plates of the cars on the grounds. The elderly people are in the majority although you hear the shouts of many youngsters romping on the beaches and on the swings in the woods. Strangers are received courteously. But the residents seem to know instinctively whether or not the stranger "belongs."

You see at Lily Dale an old couple, walking under the trees, a little feebly perhaps, but hand in hand. In their eyes shine some sort of an inner peace they have found in the old "City of Light."

Then you see the big bulletin board with its blatant signs: "trumpet seance, trance clairvoyance" and the like—and you wonder.

The road to Jamestown winds through the green hills of a dairying country and through tranquil villages, Sinclairville, settled by Yorkshire English, and Gerry, birthplace of General John M. Schofield, after whom the barracks near Honolulu are named. The annual rodeo for the benefit of the village fire department had pitched its tents in Gerry. It is a big event annually in that countryside.

On Gerry's main street, I saw a familiar figure in a sombrero, that of Colonel Jim Eskew, boss of the rodeo, which also shows annually in Rochester.

Chapter 8

Chautauqua Lake, "Bag Tied in the Middle"

Stretching diagonally across the southwestern corner of the New York State map is a big patch of blue, shaped like an hour glass. Its upper and lower halves are broad and uniform. Its midsection is as slim as the wasp waist of an 1890 belle. That blue patch on the map is the lake which the Indians named Chautauqua, "bag tied in the middle."

Chautauqua, one of the most famous of America's inland lakes, is 20 square miles of spring-fed water. It also is beauty, history, tradition, recreation and culture.

It is a Summer haven for thousands, a year-around playground, too. It is the paradise of the fisherman, the home of the tiger muskalonge. For 80 Summers culture-seeking Americans have flocked to this lakeside to drink from the fountain of knowledge that is the world-famous Chautauqua Institution.

Chautauqua Lake is framed by lush green hills and ringed by Summer cottages, hotels, amusement parks and halls of learning. Every Fourth of July eve it is ringed with fire—the red flares of the cottagers around its 50 miles of shoreline.

It is 18 miles from its head which rests on the old county seat village of Mayville to its foot which touches the industrial city of Jamestown. It is two miles across at its widest part and only a few hundred feet wide at the "narrows" in its center, where since 1811 a ferry has linked Stow on the west with Bemus Point on the east.

The lake is 1,308 feet above sea level. Once it was called the highest navigable body of water on the continent. It is only six miles from Lake Erie but 726 feet above it. The hills of the divide bar its waters from the nearby Great Lake and send them coursing southward to the faraway Gulf of Mexico via the rivers.

The Indians knew this old lake well and left many relics of their culture around its shores. Their moccasined feet beat a trail from Lake Erie over "the Hog's Back" to the head of the lake that looks like "a bag tied in the middle." This was the portage trail over which they carried the war canoes. The pioneers traveled on the frozen lake in Winter. In Summer boats and canoes carried their household goods to the cabins.

Long ago the picturesque steamboats left most of the inland lakes. But the old *City of Jamestown* still plies Chautauqua waters, although no longer on a regular run. It makes chartered trips and when I was in Jamestown in the Summer of 1953, it was at its dock, being renovated.

The first steamboat on the lake was the side-wheeler, *Chautauqua*, launched in 1828. After her came a long procession of steamers which carried both freight and passengers and touched at all the ports between Jamestown and Mayville, at Bemus Point, Maple Springs, Midway Park, Dewittville, Point Chautauqua and Hartfield Bay on the east and the Chautauqua Assembly, Stow and Lakewood on the west. In 1890 12 passenger steamboat lines were operating on the lake. Then the automobile came and stilled the paddle wheels. The lake steamers went into eternal drydock, all but the sturdy old *City of Jamestown*.

Tragedy rode the lake on the afternoon of August 14, 1872 when the steamboat *Chautauqua*, with 30 aboard, was turning into Whitney's Bay on the west side of the lake about midway between Mayville and Bemus Point. A boiler exploded, the boat was ripped to pieces and the air was showered with flying metal and timber. The casualty list was eight killed and 15 seriously injured.

Gone are the huge wooden ice houses around the lake and the ice harvests, a major Winter industry in the days of yore.

There has been racing on Chautauqua Lake since the time of the Indians. Boatmen come from all over the land to this inland lake. The Chautauqua Lake Yacht Club, based at Lakewood, has been host to international sailing events including the 1949 Snipe Regatta. A power boat regatta is an annual affair. The shores teem with Summer-long activity for all form of lake craft.

An uncontested race stirred up more excitement than any other in the history of the lake. All roads led to Mayville on October 16, 1870. There the rowing race of the century was to be staged between Charles E. Courtney of Cornell crew fame and Ed Hanlon. The event was a promotion stunt staged by Asa T. Soule, a Rochester patent medicine magnate whose chief product was a concoction known as "Hop Bitters."

Fifteen thousand people, a bevy of gamblers and pickpockets among them, descended upon quiet Mayville. They came by boat, by train, in carriages and afoot. They filled the hotels. When race time came, Courtney reported his two boats had been sawed in two during the night. So Hanlon rowed the race alone and pocketed the $6,000 stake. The incident did not add to the prestige of Courtney. Some claimed he had developed cold feet and had his own boats disabled, rather than face Hanlon.

Fishing on Chautauqua Lake, like boating, goes back to the Indian time. One version of the origin of the name has Chautauqua translated as "where the fish were taken out."

Certainly many fish have been taken out during the years. Some of them have been big ones.

But the queen of the finny tribe, Minnie the Muskie alias Minnie Methuselah, aged 20 and $42\frac{1}{2}$ inches long, is still at large. There's a price on her head. In 1930 Minnie was caught in the nets of state conservation department men and was released after being stripped of her eggs. But not before a metal tag, State Conservation Department No. 230, had been fastened to her dorsal fin. In the Spring of 1947 the old gal showed up again in the state nets and again she was relieved of her eggs and freed. Jamestown merchants have offered various prizes to the angler who hooks the old queen.

At Prendergast Point on the west side of the lake is the largest muskalonge hatchery in the world. The largest muskie caught in recent years in the lake weighed 42 pounds and was a 54 inch-long tiger. The lake also, abounds, according to Chamber of Commerce publicity, in small mouth bass, calicoes, bullheads and perch.

Lakewood on the southwest shore, now virtually a suburb of Jamestown, was "the Saratoga of the East," a fashionable Summer colony, in the 1890s. Her immense wooden hotels, the Kent and the Sterlingworth, long since departed, were frequented by wealthy Cincinnati people in steamboat days.

Fire in 1902 destroyed another landmark of the lakeside, the five-story Grand Hotel, which was built by the Baptist Association in 1877 at Point Chautauqua in an attempt to rival the Assembly Grounds of Methodist origin across the lake.

Many of the big old hotels are gone. There are plenty of hotels left and plenty of life around the lake that is shaped like an hour glass. There are serene resort colonies and lively ones, and at the foot of the lake the lights of Celoron Park, the Coney Island of the area, blaze out of nights. And thousands ride the roller coaster and dance in the vast pier ballroom, sometimes to the music of name bands.

* * *

Few county seats were named after a babe in arms. But such was the case of Mayville, shire town of Chautauqua County. At a meeting called to select a name for the settlement, Mrs. Paul Busti, wife of a land agent, walked into the room with a baby in her arms. Someone inquired the infant's name. "May," replied the mother. So they named the village at the head of Chautauqua Lake Mayville.

The three commissioners who picked the county seat site in 1808 had to drive a hemlock post in the forest to mark the spot. It also was the site picked by the Holland Land Company for its headquarters and despite the agonized howls of the established village of Canadaway (Fredonia) that the chosen site was only "a hole in the woods," Mayville got the county seat and has kept it all these years.

The present court house with the stately pillars and the greenish dome was built on its historic hill in 1909. The first courthouse of frame rose there in 1815. Beside it stood the land office and thereby hangs a tale of agrarian revolt.

In 1835 the Holland Land Company sold some of its lands to other speculators and the settlers upon those lands were compelled, when they renewed their contracts, to pay a certain sum per acre in addition to their regular payments and interests. This exaction known as the Genesee Tariff aroused intense resentment. Mass meetings were held and committees presented their grievances to the land barons but got no satisfaction.

On February 6, 1836, some 300 settlers assembled at an inn in Hartfield and above the confused welter of talk and threats sounded the firm voice of sturdy old Nathan Cheney. Leaning on a sledstake, the old man shouted: "Those who are going to Mayville with me fall in line."

Most of the crowd fell in behind Cheney and marched to the land office at Mayville, armed with axes, crowbars and hoop poles. They cut down the posts of the land office and toppled the two-story plank building. They battered down the door of the stone vault with one of the building's pillars. They pried open the iron safe and took out the papers they found there, took them in a sleigh to Hartfield where they burned them.

But they did not get all the records. William Peacock, the land agent, had heard of the advancing mob and had fled with some of the papers to the residence of Donald MacKenzie, a former governor general of the Hudson Bay Company, on the hill where Mayville Central School stands today. The story goes that when the mob went to the MacKenzie home after the land agent, the giant Scot barred the door and thundered: "If you want Peacock, you'll have to get by me first," and that the cowed mob went away.

William Peacock lost his land agent job and a suave young man from Auburn named William Henry Seward took over. He rescinded the obnoxious Genesee Tariff and the farmers lived more or less happily ever after.

The old stone vault still stands on the court house lawn and the vines grow thickly over it. The iron safe and the accounts that William Peacock saved are in Seward's old office in the History Center at Westfield. The mansion that Land Agent Peacock built in 1814 beside the court house now is the William Peacock Hotel. Mayville isn't a big town. Its population is only 1,492 but it is rich in history.

For many years Mayville was the home of Albion Winegar Tourgee, author, soldier and jurist. He borrowed the name and setting of a well known tavern on the Mayville-Westfield Road for his novel, *Button's Inn*. After the Civil War Tourgee went South and as a judge in North Carolina helped break the power of the Ku Klux Klan. His books, *A Fool's Errand* and *Bricks Without Straw*, dealt with reconstruction problems and were widely read in their time.

* * *

A natural wonder of the region, the Panama Rocks, are eight miles south of Chautauqua Lake on Route 74, on the edge of the village of Panama, which incidentally was the birthplace of James H. McGraw, co-founder of the big McGraw-Hill publishing house.

The massive and fantastically shaped Panama Rocks are remnants of a geological upheaval of millions of years ago. Trails lead through the caves, crevices and towering rocks which are shaded by trees whose exposed and twisted roots add to the weirdness of the scene.

Most of the rocks bear signs with their names on them. A boat-shaped rock is the Mayflower. Around the Python Rock grows a tree limb like a coiled snake. A narrow aperture is Fat Man's Misery. Most aptly named of all is the Giant's Casket. That big oblong boulder looks for all the world like a funeral bier with green ferns growing at its foot as a floral tribute.

Chapter 9

Citadel of Culture

It was the Chautauqua of the circuit tents pitched along thousands of village main streets in bygone Summers that made the old Indian name a household word in the America of the first quarter of this century.

That brand of Chautauqua lived spectacularly but briefly. When 1930 rolled around, the brown tents, first raised in 1903, were furled forever. The mobile Chautauquas had been on the skids since their peak year of 1924. In their time they made their impact on the thinking of rural America and swept away many cobwebs of provincialism.

They live in the memories of those who knew them—the brown tents, the green benches, the advance ballyhoo, the college boy tent crews, the golden voices of William Jennings Bryan, of Dr. Russell H. Conwell and his "Acres of Diamonds," of Galli-Curci and the Jubilee Singers—memories of the bellringers and the yodelers, the magicians, the Gilbert and Sullivan casts, the Shakespearean actors, the college presidents, the pundits, the elocutionists and the rest of "the talent" that traveled from village to village in the heyday of the tent Chautauquas.

During those years, old Mother Chautauqua on the shores of a calm blue Upstate lake, went its serene way, ignoring the noisy upstart that had borrowed its name and its program, without its ideals.

The Chautauqua Institution, founded in 1874 on Chautauqua Lake on a firm rock of religious idealism and dedicated to cultural enrichment of a people, had absolutely no connection with the Chautauqua circuits whose tents blossomed in the hinterlands from 1903 to 1930.

Each year 50,000 people pass through the gates of the fenced-in 300 acres on a wooded point of Chautauqua Lake. They come for entertainment and instruction, for intellectual stimulation and for relaxation in quiet surroundings and among mannerly people.

The Summer fare at Chautauqua is a star-studded program of music, drama and lectures. Metropolitan Opera stars sing the leads for the Chautauqua Opera Association. There are concerts by the Chautauqua Symphony Orchestra, recruited from the major symphonies of the nation. The speakers are leaders in their fields. Six Presidents of the United States have spoken at Chautauqua. The thespians of the Cleveland Play House appear in the Repertory Theater. Syracuse University conducts the 36-course Summer school, oldest in America.

A Chautauqua program is so packed with events and courses that it is almost bewildering. But always you will note the emphasis on religion.

All this began with a two-weeks Summer training school for Sunday-School teachers and on former Methodist camp meeting grounds. It was conceived by two bearded pillars of Methodism but from the first it has been interdenominational.

One founding father was a minister who later became a bishop, the Rev. John Heyl Vincent. He was head of the Sunday-School Union of his church, editor of a Sunday School journal and originator of a systematic Bible study course.

The other pioneer was a rich Akron, Ohio, inventor and

manufacturer of farm machinery, Lewis Miller, whose daughter in later years married another inventor named Thomas A. Edison. Miller was an official of the Methodist group which in 1868 had begun holding Summer camp meetings at Fair Point on Chautauqua Lake. He shared Vincent's ideas on more adequate Sunday School teacher training, without the emotional excitement of the religious camp meeting which both abhorred.

Two hundred attended that first assembly in 1874. They lived in tents and a few cottages. The initial session was pronounced a success.

A gate fee was charged and a high fence erected around the grounds. Both are still maintained, although the fee and the fence have changed with the years. In the old days most people came to Chautauqua by steamboat. Then the trolleys and the automobile came and the old back gate by the highway became the front door.

The Sunday School assembly expanded into a lyceum, with distinguished speakers. In 1876 a Scientific Congress was held and that was a radical step for a religious assembly. That same year the Temperance Congress convened, starring its high priestess, Frances E. Willard. An added attraction in the early years was a large model of Palestine, 360 feet long, with cities, Dead Sea and all, which was laid out along the lake near the present Miller Bell Tower.

In 1878 Doctor Vincent inaugurated the Chautauqua Literary and Scientific Circle, a course in guided home study, which in its first decade enrolled 80,000, many of them dwellers in villages and on farms. This was the forerunner of the book clubs, the University Extension movement and the correspondence schools. The CLSC shrank with the years but its Recognition Day, its commencement, has become a tradition. The classes gather at the gate of the sacred St.

Paul's Grove, the gate that is opened only once a year, and with their banners and their music march into the Hall of Philosophy, while girls in white scatter flowers in their path.

In the late 1870s and 80s came the Teachers' Retreat, the School of Languages and the School of Theology. The Chautauqua Idea was sprouting in many directions. In 1883 the educational projects were merged into the Chautauqua University, chartered to give degrees. In 1900 it relinquished that right and in 1902 all Chautauqua activities were incorporated into the Chautauqua Institution.

The first Summer School in the United States came into flower in 1883 under the leadership of a young teacher of Hebrew, Dr. William Rainey Harper, who later became president of Chicago University.

In 1877 S. L. Greene, a deaf mute, addressed a large audience under the trees in the first outdoor auditorium and in the sign language. There was a burst of hand clapping as he closed. Doctor Vincent told the assemblage: "The speaker is unable to hear your applause. Let us wave our handkerchiefs instead of clapping hands." Like a sea of white lilies, the handkerchiefs danced under the maples. Thus was born the Chautauqua Salute, most famous of all the Chautauqua traditions.

It is used sparingly. The accolade is never given save at the direction of the head of the Institution. At the annual Old First Night when tribute is paid to the memory of departed Chautauquans, the handkerchiefs raised high in the salute are allowed to descend slowly in drooping fashion. Another less picturesque but more practical ceremony of Old First Night is the announcement of gifts. At the 1953 "Community Gift Ceremony," $80,000 was pledged.

At the opening of the assembly on a Sunday, usually around July 4, the president of the Institution raps a gavel thrice and then he repeats the same words Doctor Vincent used at the first assembly in 1874.

One of the first to ascend the Chautauqua rostrum was Frank Beard, who gave "chalk talks." After him came a procession that reads like a section of "Who's Who"—Susan B. Anthony, Edward Everett Hale, Julia Ward Howe, Jane Addams, Helen Keller, Charles W. Eliot, "Old Bob" La-Follette, William Jennings Bryan, Norman Thomas, Admiral Richard E. Byrd, to name a few. All shades of opinion in that cavalcade.

Ulysses S. Grant was the first of seven Presidents to visit Chautauqua but the General didn't speak. He came to talk over old times with his former pastor at Galena, Ill., the Rev. John H. Vincent. Franklin D. Roosevelt made his famous "I hate war" speech at Chautauqua in 1936.

Thomas A. Edison courted his wife, the daughter of Lewis Miller, at Chautauqua. His widow for years was a supporter of Chautauqua projects, notably the Bird and Tree Club. Alonzo Stagg was captain of the baseball team in the 1890s on which William Lyon Phelps played. Alexander Woollcott, John H. Finley and Ida M. Tarbell worked on Chautauqua papers.

From a few tents and wooden cottages, an old hotel and a speaker's stand on the terraced terrain of a former camp meeting site sprang the present Chautauqua Institution, a veritable city, with its great amphitheater, roofed but not enclosed, seating 7,000; its Norton Memorial Hall where the operas and plays are offered; its many public buildings and religious edifices, its hotels, some of them huge; its boarding houses and its 500 private homes, some of them betraying the Victorian lineage of the place, along narrow shady streets that were laid out in horse and buggy days and that know few automobiles.

From the beginning Chautauqua was a non-profit institution. Its founders decreed that all funds remaining after expenses were paid should be put into improvement of the property and expansion of the program. It has relied through the years mostly on the generosity of those who love Chautauqua and want to keep the light of popular knowledge burning there.

The depression all but quenched the light. In 1934 the organization went into a friendly receivership. It was $800,000 in debt and there were three Summers to pay it off. The Save Chautauqua Fund was launched on a nation-wide basis. The present head of the Institution, Samuel M. Hazlett, a Pittsburgh lawyer, led the campaign. And the last check came in on the last day of the 1936 season. Chautauqua was saved.

During its eight weeks of activity, Chautauqua is not a Summer St. Petersburg, Fla., a haven for old retired folks, as some people seem to think. There are lots of young people at Chautauqua and all kinds of recreational facilities, even for the youngest. Crew cuts and youthful hair-dos mingle with the gray and silver in every assemblage. And it is mostly the younger folks who flock to the University Summer schools, the music school, the writers' workshop and the other halls of learning.

Chautauqua, for all its activities, has an air of serenity. It seems removed from the market place and the money changers. "Education and Recreation" is its slogan. People seem relaxed and content. They are having a good time—in a mannerly way—and at the same time are satisfying their thirst for knowledge. They come from far and near and some of them come year after year, generation after generation.

There are rules and regulations on the assembly grounds. Some of them are the kind that most people would like to have enforced in their own neighborhoods but can't. Automobile traffic is restricted. Noise is not tolerated at night. Dogs are not welcomed and must be leashed. And cats are taboo—because of the Bird and Tree Club.

Chautauqua is more than a place. It is an Idea. For 80 years it has been a strong educational force in America. It has never departed from the spiritual ideals upon which it was founded nor lost its tolerantly religious flavor. On July and August Sundays the great ampitheater is crowded with 7,000 people of all religious faiths. They listen each Sunday to a minister of a different denomination. Religious unity is not the least of the facets of many-sided Chautauqua.

Theodore Roosevelt once called Chautauqua "the most American place in America." That was a pretty broad statement. There are all kinds of Americans. Celoron Park, the Coney Island of the bright lights, down the road a few miles, is just as American—for those who prefer that type of entertainment and environment.

Chapter 10

The Town That James Built

James Prendergast saw gold in the rough, steep hills of glacial drift when first he visited the foot of Chautauqua Lake in the year 1806.

The gold was not in the earth. It was in the dense forests of virgin white pine which covered it. James Prendergast looked at the streams that ran swiftly through the woods in those days—the lake outlet, called the Rapids, and the old Indian river Chadakoin—and he visioned saw mills on their banks and lumber floating on their waters.

He was 41 and a bachelor then. He had come from his home in Pittston, now Honeoye, in Ontario County, to visit his parents who had settled near Mayville. The Prendergasts were a numerous tribe and they were early settlers in Chautauqua. But it was James's settlement that grew into an opulent city and which bears his given name today.

In 1809 he bought 1,000 acres of that rough land which had caught his fancy three years before. He was married now and in 1810 he brought his family from Pittston. In 1811 they moved into the comfortable log house he had built beside the Rapids and the Chadakoin. That same year he built a dam and a saw mill at the Sprague Street bridge, the first of Jamestown's many industries.

A little lumber camp of 13 families sprang up along the river and it was called Prendergast Mills or just the Rapids.

It was a forbidding place with its uneven hills, its sloughs and quicksands. A rope was kept handy in every cabin to extricate the humans, animals and vehicles that got mired in the swamps. The flats known as the "Big Fly" was a breeding place for fever and the ague.

More saw mills rose beside the streams and the Durham boats and rafts began carrying the lumber down the rivers. Gradually the swamps were drained and filled and the rough hills smoothed down in places. There really wasn't much that could be done about the hills.

The little saw mill town expanded. In 1812 Eleazer Daniels opened a blacksmith shop. That was the beginning of what was to be the community's major industry 140 years later, metal fabrication. In 1813 Phineas Palmiter's chair shop filled its first order, a dozen pieces for the new frame home of James Prendergast. That was the start of Jamestown's famed furniture industry. In 1816 Daniel Hazeltine founded the first woolen mill and Jamestown's third basic industry, textiles, was born.

In 1815 the Rapids cut three million feet of boards, most of which were rafted down the rivers. It deserved an official name and it got one—Jamestown, after James Prendergast.

The father of the community became the first supervisor of the town of Ellicott, the first judge of the court of special pleas, Jamestown's first postmaster. He sold his Jamestown holdings in 1836. There had been gold in those rough hills. He retired with a comfortable fortune to his big country estate at Kiantone, south of the town of James. His name is perpetuated in the Prendergast Memorial Library, given the city by a descendant.

In the 1820s Jamestown's industry became more diversified, although still based on the forest timber. Besides the saw mills, factories along the river were turning out chairs, bedsteads, cabinets, sash, scythe snaths, pails and tubs, all kinds of wooden ware.

From that Jamestown blossomed into the leading furniture manufacturing center in the East, second only to Grand Rapids in the nation. At first all operations were by hand. This industry always has demanded skilled craftsmen. For many years all the furniture was made from the native wood. Now luxury wood is shipped into the plants of Jamestown.

For many years the products of the local factories were in display in plants, stores and hotels for the benefit of the buyers who stopped off in Jamestown on their way to and from the Grand Rapids furniture fairs. In 1917 the Jamestown furniture industry built the nine-story Furniture Exposition Building in Second Street, where twice a year is held a furniture mart which draws buyers from all the country.

A trend in recent years has been toward metal furniture. Jamestown is still the furniture capital of the East but the making of wooden furniture no longer is its banner industry. The metal fabrication industry, and that includes the manufacture of metal furniture, holds the crown today. Third in line in the textile industry, with two large worsted mills.

The chances are about 9 to 1 that when you go to the polls on primary and election days, you will pull the lever of a voting machine made in Jamestown. The Automatic Voting Machine Company in Jamestown for years has made the great majority of those used in the United States.

The Erie Railroad came to town in 1860 under the name of the Atlantic and Great Western in response to Jamestown's clamor over being left off the main line. It built its tracks on the flatlands along the Chadakoin River. In that "Industrial Valley" besides the tracks and the river, stretching from the old Rapids the length of the city and into the busy suburb of Falconer, is a continuous line of factories. It is an awe-inspiring sight, that long procession like soldiers drawn up on parade with smoky plumes.

An industrial city with a sound economy is Jamestown, largest of the cities in the Western counties in the Southern Tier, with a population of nearly 44,000, of whom more than half are of Swedish descent.

Its concentration of industry in the narrow valley is typical of Jamestown's progressive and practical ways. On the tiers of hills above the Industrial Valley are the residential streets with their brick pavements and many shade trees. On the northern tier just above the tracks and the river and the plants is a compact and busy shopping area.

Here is a brisk and friendly city, a city of locally-owned industries in the main; a city of homes, most of them owned by their occupants; a "money-in-the bank" city. It also is a city of considerable culture, with its Little Theater, its symphony orchestra, its civic music association and its civic forum. It is a progressive city, one which pioneered in municipal ownership of its utilities.

Its old sobriquet, now in the discard although a few old business firms retain it, was the Pearl City. In many ways it is the Pearl of the Southern Tier. Year after year its Falcons have made a farce out of the PONY League race. At this writing Jamestown is leading its nearest rival by 20 games.

* * *

A friend said to me when I told him I was off for Jamestown: "You will find nothing but hills and Swedes in Jimtown."

The hills are still there, just as they were in James Prendergast's day, although the virgin forest and the swamps are gone. On those hills has been built a bustling city—maybe in spite of the hills.

The Swedes are there, more than 20,000 of them and perhaps "Jimtown" is the solid and opulent town it is largely because of them. They brought to the foot of Chautauqua Lake many progressive ideas of their homeland, along with their native traits of industry, thrift and stability.

They are in every field of community life. They have their own organizations but they are not clannish. A visitor to Jamestown notes the Swedish flavor of the town only in the sign, "Kaffestugen," on a downtown coffee shop, two solid pages of Andersons in the telephone directory and the many natural blondes on the street.

The Scandinavian invasion began in 1849 when two young women, Johanna Johnson and Lisa Anderson, came to Jamestown from a little Swedish colony at Sugar Grove, Pa., just over the state border. They married and had children. Many other Swedes joined them in the 1850's and they kept coming through the years. The men were skilled craftsmen and they readily found work in the furniture shops and other industries.

One of them for years influenced the course of his city. Samuel A. Carlson is his name. He is in his eighties now and still interested in the affairs of the city of which he was mayor for 28 years. From the day he came down from Swede Hill as a new alderman, he fought for municipal ownership and other reforms. First he won lower electricity rates. Then he sought general use of the municipal steam generated electric plant which had been set up in 1890 but which supplied power only for street lights. In 1894 the city purchased the equipment that led to the present muncipally owned and operated electric system.

That came about only over the bitter opposition of the

privately owned utility. In 1903 the privately owned water plant became municipally owned. Some called Sam Carlson Socialistic but he never gave up his battle for municipal ownership. In 1920 he vainly sought to wrest from Dan Reed the seat in Congress which that doughty Dunkirk Republican still holds.

Only two New York State governors came from the four western counties of the Southern Tier. One was Frank Higgins of Olean. The other was Reuben E. Fenton of Jamestown. Fenton was born near Frewsburg and took up residence in nearby Jamestown after he made a fortune in lumbering operations.

He served in Congress as an anti-slavery Democrat before the Civil War, then joined the GOP. He was twice elected governor and then went to the United States Senate. He was a suave, tall man with an impressive iron gray beard, no orator but a shrewd political manipulator. He met his match when he tried to wrest control of the state Republican machine from Roscoe Conkling. When the Liberal Republicans in 1872 nominated Horace Greeley for President, Reuben Fenton was a leader of the splinter party. He had no other place to go. He died while attending a meeting of bank directors in Jamestown. One of Jamestown's two big hotels today is the Governor Fenton. The other is the Hotel Jamestown.

Probably the most famous living son (or foster son) of Jamestown is Robert Houghwout Jackson, associate justice of the United States Supreme Court. He was born over the state line in Spring Creek, Pa., and spent his boyhood in Frewsburg, where his father ran a hotel and livery stable. On graduation from law school, he hung out his shingle in Jamestown. His chief client was the street railway company.

Bob Jackson was a leading Democrat in a Republican

stronghold and when the New Deal came into power, he was rewarded with the job of general counsel for the Internal Revenue Bureau. The brilliant, dark haired, slim young Jamestown lawyer came under the eye of Franklin D. Roosevelt. Jackson became FDR's "fair-haired boy." The President wanted to make him governor of New York.

But the bosses told FDR Jackson was not well enough known among the voters. So he went up the ladder of New Deal officialdom—assistant attorney general, solicitor-general, attorney general and finally the highest court in the land. Justice Jackson won international attention as the chief counsel for the United States at the trials of the Nazi war criminals, Goering and Ribbentrop among them. He has gone a long way from the farm at Spring Creek.

Two big league pitchers, Hugh Bedient and Ray "Bugs" Caldwell, came from Jamestown. So did Lucille Ball, movie and television ("I Love Lucy") star. She frequently visits her home city. Perhaps she is better known to the average American today than is Mr. Justice Jackson.

* * *

In a cool and sylvan wood, seven miles southwest of Jamestown, in the town of Kiantone and smack on the state line, a century ago stood the bizarre "City of Harmonia," ruled by the shades of the departed great, with Benjamin Franklin as its celestial mayor.

The founder of that colony was a Yankee mystic, a Spiritualist medium, John Murray Spear. The mineral springs at Kiantone with their supposedly magic medicinal properties attracted Spear to the site. In his Utopia there was to be complete freedom of opinion and conduct. The heavenly rulers, among them Jefferson, Socrates, Martin Luther and John

Adams, revealed their wishes to their earthly agent, John Murray Spear.

Men and women came to live and to practice strange rites in the seven curious circular wooden buildings which rose in the grove in 1853. The countryside was aghast over the goings-on there. By the light of flaring torches and clad in white robes, the cultists tunneled into a hillside, looking in vain for the buried treasure of a prehistoric web-footed tribe. They did come upon a fresh water spring.

The Utopians devised a mysterious perpetual motion machine, into which "a matron of the colony breathed life into the metal framework while enduring the pangs of child birth," according to a contemporary account. The machine was moved to the Randolph barn of Thad Sheldon, a leading Spearite. Outraged villagers broke in and smashed it one night.

Finally internal dissension and the hostility of its neighbors ended the most fantastic colony ever known in the Southern Tier. Now there are a few Summer cabins in the woods where stood the lost City of Harmonia and its story belongs to the folklore of the land.

Chapter 11

Cattaraugus, High, Wide and Handsome

Cattaraugus is 1,385 square miles and 78,000 square people.

It also is oil and Indians and "the cattle upon a thousand hills." The oil is along its southern borders. The Indians are on two reservations, one along the Allegheny River, the other along the Cattaraugus Creek.

The hills are everywhere. In the north they are rolling yet mighty. In the south along the state line they are mountains. And I am going to call them mountains. The historian Schoolcraft once likened Cattaraugus' succession of hills and vales to "a piece of rumpled calico."

In this "calico land" lived a prehistoric, mound-building people before the Senecas, the Nation of the Hill, came to drive out the Eries, the Nation of the Cat, and in turn were driven out by the paleface people. Almost every corner of Cattaraugus has yielded its relics of Indian occupancy.

Cattaraugus is an Indian name which means "foul-smelling banks," hardly a lovely connotation. It originates from the natural gas the wondering Indians found oozing from the soil along the Cattaraugus Creek. But it was along the serpentine Allegheny that the white men tapped the rich oil sands in the depths of the rocky earth.

The Indian names are still upon this rumpled land—names of streams like the Conewango and the Tunegawant—names of places like Gowanda, Ischua and Kill Buck.

Cattaraugus County is part of the three-million acre tract that the shrewd Dutch capitalists who formed the Holland Land Company bought from land-poor Robert Morris in 1793. It was established on March 11, 1808, the same day that Chautauqua was created. But it was not until 1817 that the first court session was held in Olean, the mother town. Ellicottville was the county seat until 1868 when Little Valley became the shire town.

Cattaraugus has two cities, Olean, prophetically given a name that means "oil," and Salamanca, the railroad center that is the only city in the world on an Indian reservation. There are also two "Rock Cities" in the county, not to mention a "Breathing Well," a "Checkered Schoolhouse" and the largest of all New York State parks.

The pioneers cut down the virgin forests and lumbering ceased to be a major industry. The oil fields are restricted to the southern borders of Cattaraugus. Dairying always has been the backbone of its economy. It is a land flowing with much milk and some honey where graze "the cattle upon a thousand hills."

Chapter 12

Olean and Oil

When Adam Hoops, veteran of the Revolution, started a settlement in the dark pine woods of Southwestern New York in 1804, he envisoned a great river port there.

It was at the head of navigation on the Allegheny River, in a time when the rivers were major routes of trade and travel. The Allegheny merged with the mightier Ohio at Pittsburgh, the gateway to the burgeoning West. Adam Hoops dreamed of a stream of river traffic and of commercial glory for his port in the virgin forest.

The Allegheny is one of the most picturesque streams in America. The mountains in the background, the green of its banks and its little islands give it a wild beauty all its own. But in its northern reaches the river was too narrow, too winding, too shallow, too full of rocks and shoals for any craft larger than the lumber rafts. And they could descend the river only when the Spring thaws came. Then the Erie Canal was dug, far to the north, opening a new and splendid highway to the West. The river traffic was doomed and the dream faded.

Little did Adam Hoops know it but a name he picked—or coined—in 1804 was prophetic. That name was Olean. It is a corruption of the Latin word, "oleum," which means *oil*.

For Olean's destiny lay not in the river nor in the pine forests. It lay in the underground treasure along the state line. It was the oil, pumped from the rocky hills and valleys and piped into the refineries and storage tanks of Olean that made it one of the leading cities of the Southern Tier. Development of the Cattaraugus oil fields, an extension of the rich Bradford, Pa., pool, after the Civil War laid the bedrock of Olean's prosperity. Fortunes founded on oil, the "Pennsylvania crude," finest in the market, built most of the business blocks along broad Union Street and the big houses on the shady side avenues.

Today Olean is a city of diversified industry, a solid, eye-pleasing and home-like city of 22,000, on the winding river and in the shadow of the mountains, the kind of a place that makes the tourist say: "This would be a good town to live in."

* * *

Adam Hoops and three associates in 1803 contracted for the first tract sold by the Holland Land Company in what is now Cattaraugus County, 20,000 acres at the junction of the Allegheny and what is now Olean Creek, then known as the Ischua.

The settlement begun there in 1804 was the first in Cattaraugus County, other than the Quaker mission opened on the Indian Reservation in 1798. That year of 1804 Adam Hoops coined the name, Olean. In a letter to Joseph Ellicott, agent for the Holland Land Company, he wrote that "the neighborhood of the oil spring [the famous Seneca spring near Cuba] suggests a name . . . which I wish to adopt. It is Olean."

So the place where Olean Creek empties into the Allegheny became known as Olean Point and a famous and busy place it was in the early days. Major Hoops gave the name of Alexander Hamilton to the village he laid out south of the Point. But the name did not stick and was soon dropped.

The village and the Point which it absorbed became Olean.

The Hoops venture soon ran into financial shoals. The ambitious major lost his tract through foreclosure when he failed to make his payments to the land company. The bachelor father of Olean left for West Chester, Pa., where he died in 1845, a disappointed, broken man.

But he left his imprint on the river town he founded in the broad, straight streets he laid out and in the names of fellow officers in the Revolution that he gave those streets—names like Sullivan, Greene, Henley and Laurens. He set aside the public square, now called Lincoln Park, in the heart of Olean and boulders there honor his memory and that of his brother and associate, Robert.

Olean is the mother town of Cattaraugus. When the county was set up in 1808, its whole territory was the Town of Olean. The first courts were held in Olean in 1817. When in 1818 the courts were moved to Ellicottville, disgruntled Olean people who had business in the new shire town brought tents and provisions with them and camped in the open, rather than spend any money in Ellicottville. The nights were cool and the economic boycott did not last long.

In 1807 the Allegheny River was declared a public highway and that year the first raft went down the river, the forerunner of thousands.

For 15 years after 1810, every Spring saw a multitude of emigrants assembled at Olean, bound for the West via the Allegheny and the Ohio. When the ice melted and the thaws swelled the river, they would depart on huge rafts. Raft building was a considerable industry at Olean in those days.

Some years the emigrants outnumbered the normal population of the place. They overflowed the old Boat House, Ebenezer Reed's tavern, and had to live in tents and shanties. Some seasons when the wait for high water on the river was extra long, the emigrants ran out of provisions and there was suffering among them.

The high tide of emigration was reached in 1818 when 3,000 went down the river, 350 of them on a single raft. After the Erie Canal was completed in 1825, Olean ceased to be a point of embarkation for the West and its importance as a port declined.

But until the virgin stands of pine and hemlock were depleted, the big rafts continued to carry logs and lumber down the Allegheny. Ten of these platforms 16 feet square would be hooked together and, piled high with lumber, would shove off for Pittsburgh. The river widens at Warren, Pa., and there three of these 10 raft units would be joined together for the rest of the journey to Pittsburgh in what became known as an Allegheny fleet. Millions of feet of lumber were floated down the river and rafting continued on the Allegheny into the second half of the 19th Century.

Grandiose plans for making the northern Allegheny navigable—at federal expense—have bobbed up periodically but none of them was realized. In all history only two steamboats have docked at Olean. One was the *Allegheny,* a sternwheel packet which came up river from Pittsburgh in 1830, and the other was the *Newcastle,* with a capacity of 80 passengers, which tied up in 1837.

The success of the Erie Canal, with its ill effects on the economy of the Southern Tier, brought immediate agitation for a canal which would link the Clinton Ditch and the Allegheny River.

In 1836 the state waterway was begun from Rochester to Olean. It was 20 years before it reached Olean. Then it was extended to Mill Grove and the slackwater of the Allegheny in the town of Portville. In 1878 it was abandoned as unprofitable.

In its time, the old Genesee Valley Canal and a rival which appeared in 1851, the Erie Railroad, quickened Olean's commercial tempo. New capital was attracted to the village. Tanneries and other new industries arrived.

Then came the oil derricks, the pumps, the pipe lines and the storage tanks and a new and spectacular chapter in the story of Olean. The town on the banks of the Allegheny fulfilled the destiny written for it in the stars ever since Adam Hoops had given it the name that means *oil*.

* * *

Long before a former railroad conductor named Edwin L. Drake, who had to borrow $600 for his drilling tools, made history and a fortune with his famous 1859 oil strike at Titusville, Pa., which gave birth to the commercial petroleum industry, the presence of oil in Cattaraugus and Allegany Counties was no secret. But no one had exploited it.

For centuries the Indians had been using as medicine the liquid that floated on the surface of the Seneca Oil Spring on the Reservation, only 20 miles northeast of Olean and near the Allegany County village of Cuba. A French priest made the first recorded mention of oil in America in 1627 after visiting the region, as will be told in a later chapter. For years settlers had been skimming oil for their harnesses and boots from other springs and creeks in the Southern Tier.

The Titusville gusher spurred an active search for oil in the Olean area in 1861, as well as across the state line around Bradford. Two dry holes were drilled that year. A test well sunk on the northern outskirts of Olean in 1865 brought in considerable natural gas but no oil.

In 1865 Job Moses brought in the first producing commercial well in New York State, near Limestone southwest of

Olean. That same pioneer drilled two other producing wells in the same locality within a year.

A red letter event in the story of the Cattaraugus oil fields was the completion in 1875 of a pipe line, first in the state, from the pump station in the Tuna Valley near the state line to storage tanks on Academy Hill in Olean, 14 miles away.

More pipe lines followed and Olean was on the way to becoming the storage and refining center of the Cattaraugus fields, where 150 paying wells were driven in a year. Derricks were rising on all sides, among the fabulous boulders of Rock City, in the Chipmonk Run, the Four Mile Valley, at Knapp's Creek and on the Indian Reservation, where leases had been negotiated with the Seneca Nation.

All this spelled a new prosperity for Olean. The golden years were the 1880s when most of the output of the lush oil fields on both sides of the state line was stored in and shipped from Olean.

Great tank farms rose around the village (Olean did not become a city until 1893). The massing of 300 of these huge tanks, which in a decade stored a total of ten million barrels of oil, made Olean for a time the world's largest storage depot for oil. Occasional fires on these tank farms provided spectacles that were long remembered. In 1888 waning production ended the tank farms in the region. The big wrought iron tanks were cut down and shipped West.

In 1881 Standard Oil completed the first major pipe line in the United States. This six-inch line connected Olean in the heart of the producing fields with Bayonne, N. J., 315 miles away. The line was patroled by walkers who covered the 28 miles between their stations in two days. It was in constant operation until 1927, when it yielded to the competition of ocean tankers and new mid-continent fields.

Olean's first oil refinery was built in 1861. Mighty Standard set up its Acme Works in 1878. In 1902 Vacuum Oil, a major company which had been founded in Rochester in 1866, bought a refinery. The next year it merged with Acme. Today the Socony Vacuum refinery is one of Olean's major industries.

After the first flush years, oil production had been steadily declining in the New York State fields. The second decade of the new century brought a new low and wells were being junked and leases abandoned. The once rich oil belt was saved through a process, which had been accidentally discovered years before—the principle of "flooding."

By this process the oil still left in the sands is driven from one well to another by the introduction of water to create hydrostatic pressure. Under this system rows of water wells are first drilled in straight lines. After at least six months, sometimes longer, oil wells are put down in a line from a point midway between two lines of water wells to push the oil at right angles to the travel of the water.

Although this flooding process had been known and used surreptitiously for years, it was not legalized in New York State until 1919. It revitalized exhausted fields and gave the oil belt in the Southern Tier a long and steady period of high production.

That production, however, has been declining in the past six years. According to the State Department of Commerce, the fields in Cattaraugus, Allegany and Steuben (the Steuben yield is negligible) produced a total of 4,863,000 barrels in 1946. In 1951 the total was 4,143,000 barrels.

No new pools are being developed or any old ones extended and little drilling is being done because, as oil men will tell you, the high production cost leaves too little margin of profit.

But four million barrels of oil in a year isn't hay and the oil men will find a way to boost production and revive the fields, just as they did 30 years ago when flooding was introduced. They are experimenting right now with chemicals and other devices, including the use of sugar, and studying the technique of secondary flooding, not only to keep the pumps singing in the hills but to add to their chorus.

Olean's industry is really diversified. Heading the list is the Clark Bros. Co., manufacturer of compressors and diesel engines and employing 2,350. Other major plants make kitchen furniture, ceramic floors, television parts, cutlery, oil products and oil line machinery. The Pennsylvania Railroad, which has car repair shops in the city, and the Erie have sizeable payrolls. Yet despite its many industries, Olean's visage is not sooty.

Many of its public buildings are around shady Lincoln Park, the old public square whose benches sometimes holds as many "sitters" as there are in the spacious lobby of the Olean House, one of the Tier's better hotels.

Facing the park is the white mansion with the stately portico which was the residence of Frank W. Higgins, governor of New York in 1904–06. The Higgins fortune was founded on western lands and Michigan lumber. Frank Higgins was an organization Republican who was rewarded with the governorship after service in the State Senate and a term as lieutenant governor. He and his political ally, oil millionaire Nicholas V. V. Franchot, controlled the county GOP in their time.

In 1938 Capt. Frederick Way, Jr., veteran river pilot, lowered a motor boat from the Allegheny River bridge in Olean and with a companion shoved off for Pittsburgh. It was the first motor-propelled craft to traverse that difficult stream in a century. That trip provided material for Way's book, *The Allegheny,* one of the *Rivers of America* series.

Captain Way returned in the Spring of 1953 and again took off in his motor boat from Olean. This time he was bound for New Orleans and the sesquicentennial of the Louisiana Purchase, taking gifts from communities along the way. From Olean he took a small pine tree, symbolic of the lumber once shipped by river from Western New York. Some of that lumber went into New Orleans' storied French quarter. Olean also sent a container of crude oil from the Seneca Oil Spring near Cuba, which gave the city its name.

Olean in 1922 became the center of a widely publicized experiment in rural health when Cattaraugus was picked as the rural county for a health demonstration under the Milbank Memorial Fund. The experiment covered a wide field in its eight years. The Cattaraugus County Health Department, which it set up, carries on its work.

Olean has a fine large general hospital as well as a rather unusual private one, the Mountain Clinic, opened in 1917 by the region's "Mayo brothers," the pioneering physician brothers, William H. and Stephen V. Mountain.

The Allegheny, ordinarily placid and always picturesque, can be a raging devil when swollen by rain and thaw. More than once Olean people living on its banks have had to flee their homes. Sometimes they left in rowboats. In recent years United States flood control projects have been constructed, both at Olean and its comely southern neighbor, the village of Portville, which was hard hit at flood times.

Portville has many elegant homes, testifying to its onetime importance as a lumbering and tannery center. There lived the Wheelers, the Dusenburys, the Mersereaus, families long potent in business and in politics.

Leading off into the hills from the Olean-Portville Road near Weston's Mills is "The Promised Land Road." It is a phenomenon of that countryside. Along a stretch of that road the traveler gets the impression he is going down hill when actually he is going up. It is said to be an optical illusion caused by the contour of the land.

South of Olean and close to the Pennsylvania border, along the Olean-Bradford highway, which is virtually lined with oil pumps, some of which are not pumping these days, is Rock City. It is one of the wonders of the Southern Tier—of the whole East for that matter.

There strange-shaped rock formations, some of them 30 to 40 feet high, are separated by fissures or "streets" of varying width, giving the appearance of a city. The huge rocks were heaved up millions of years ago. From the Signal Rock on the city's flat top, one can get a glorious view of the wooded valley below, the village of Allegany in the distance and the mountains on the horizon.

Rock City is privately owned and the visitor pays 50 cents before he descends into its labyrinth of streets, caves and weird rock structures. To me the most amazing thing about Rock City are the pumps at its top, bringing the oil up through the rocks from a depth of 2,000 feet. The rocks form a protective covering over the oil-sands beneath them.

Oil is where you find it in the Southern Tier. Sometimes oil pumps have been set up in strange places. In the 1920s two oil wells were operating on the grounds of Olean's Bartlett Country Club.

* * *

Three miles west of Olean on Route 17, along the Allegheny River and in the shadow of the mountains is the 500-

acre campus of St. Bonaventure University, largest college of the Franciscan order in the United States, with a 100-man faculty and more than 1,200 students.

There is an Old World air about that campus with its Florentine architecture, tile roofs, the statues of the saints and the brown robes and the white cinctures of the friars.

The story of that campus goes back to 1836 and the dream of a devout Catholic land owner, Nicholas Devereux, who had bought a vast tract from the Holland Land Company in southern Cattaraugus and Allegany Counties.

On 300 acres of that tract Devereux and his associates in the Allegany City Company confidently laid out a future metropolis—on paper. It was to be the cultural and commercial hub of the area. The first survey of the Erie Railroad ran through its site. The contemplated Genesee Valley Canal was to join the Allegheny River there. The Allegheny was to be widened and deepened. On the basis of all these dreams, a large hotel was built at "Allegany City."

Father Ireaneus Herscher, OFM, librarian at St. Bonaventure, has some old maps that show the lavishness of the plans for the dream city. On these maps the largest plots are marked "Franciscan" and "college lands." From the first Devereux planned a Franciscan college there.

But the Erie Railroad changed its route. The Genesee Valley Canal swung to the eastward. The Allegheny was not widened. The paper city crumpled. There never was an Allegany City—just the old hotel which remained on the scene until a decade ago.

One part of Nicholas Devereux's brave dream did come true. The college of the friars in time did rise beside the Allegheny.

The building of the Erie Railroad brought many Catholic

workmen, many of them fresh from Ireland, to Cattaraugus County. As there were few churches or priests of their faith in the region, Devereux went to Rome, accompanied by Bishop John Timon of Buffalo, to ask the Vatican to send Franciscan missionaries to Western New York. Devereux offered $5,000 and 200 acres of land.

Four volunteers came from three Franciscan schools in Italy. Their leader was Father Pamphilius De Magliano, venerated as "Father Pamphilo," first president of St. Bonaventure.

In June of 1855, the four Brown Robes arrived at Ellicottville, the seat of the Devereux land company. John Devereux, son of Nicholas, provided a residence for the friars. With the arrival of more priests from abroad, the little community of Franciscans, first in the Eastern United States, began its work in a converted school house which had been bought for the purpose by Nicholas Devereux. It served as monastery, chapel and school. The school began with three professors and three students. Such was the humble cradle of St. Bonaventure University.

In the meantime a new monastery-school was rising on the land given by Devereux on the site of his dream city. In October, 1858, the building was completed and placed under the protection of St. Bonaventure, patron of Franciscan studies and learning. In the Spring of 1859 the college opened its doors to 15 students. The pioneer building on the campus lasted until 1930 when a two million dollar fire destroyed it, the church and the seminary.

In 1875 St. Bonaventure was incorporated as a college and on October 4, 1950 it became the first and only Franciscan educational institution in the 700-year old history of the order to be raised to university status.

Since the Fall of 1952, "St. Bona" has been co-educational. St. Elizabeth Teachers College, which trains Franciscan sisters for teaching, is in the adjacent village of Allegany. St. Bonaventure has its own postoffice.

Father Pamphilius was the first of 12 presidents of St. Bonaventure. The present head of the university is the Very Rev. Juvenal Lalor.

The names of many benefactors are on the college buildings. The largest, Devereux Hall, the main dormitory, housing 500 students, honors the memory of Nicholas Devereux. After the disastrous fire of 1930, the seminarians were crowded into Devereux Hall until the new Christ The King Seminary rose in all its dignity of Franciscan Florentine design.

The Father Joseph Butler Memorial gymnasium honors the memory of a former president. Venerable Alumni Hall was built by alumni and friends of the school. The stately library building is a memorial to Colonel Michael Friedsam of New York. The main classroom building, Lynch Hall, erected in 1900, was struck by lightning and wrecked by fire in 1935. It was rebuilt and renamed de la Roche Hall after the Franciscan who first recorded the presence of oil in the New World, at the nearby Seneca Spring. The 15,000-seat Forness Stadium was the gift of Fred Forness of Olean, a director of the university.

The names of two of baseball's all-time greats, who in the 1890s made St. Bonaventure teams feared on college diamonds, are perpetuated in St. Bona's McGraw-Jennings Athletic Field.

John J. McGraw began his professional baseball career in 1890 as a pitcher-third baseman with the Olean club of the old New York and Pennsylvania League. He was not given a chance to play regularly and as he had no contract, he soon jumped to Hornell. Before the 1890 season was over, he was wearing a Wellsville uniform. Two years later he was with the Baltimore Orioles and in the big time.

During the years 1892–95 the fiery McGraw spent his off seasons at St. Bonaventure where he was captain-coach of the baseball team. In 1893 he persuaded his more sedate Baltimore teammate, Hughie Jennings, to join him at the college. The pair attended school in the Fall and Winter, coached the college nine, then known as the Alleganys, in the Spring and played for the Orioles in the Summer. It was all perfectly legitimate in those days. Jennings was enrolled at St. Bonaventure from 1894, the year he became a Baltimore regular, until 1897. He became to the Detroit Tigers what McGraw was to the New York Giants.

In 1927 McGraw and Jennings came back to the old campus—for the dedication of the field named in their honor. McGraw brought along his New York Giants and Hornsby and Ott and the rest of his stars played the St. Bona Indians. The Giants won 11 to 2.

In recent years the emphasis has been on basketball at St. Bonaventure and Brown and White court teams are often in the annual national intercollegiate finals in New York's Madison Square Garden, battling it out with the best in the land.

For 18 years the St. Bonaventure Railroad was celebrated as the world's shortest standard gauge line. It was a little over a quarter of a mile long. After the Olean electric railway suspended operations in 1929, the college took over the spur which connected the campus with the Pennsylvania Railroad. A "dinkey" engine was purchased and until it broke down in 1940, it hauled coal and building materials.

As president of the university from 1920 to 1949, Father Thomas Plassman, now rector of Christ The King Seminary, was also president of the railroad and as such he exchanged passes with the heads of great trunk systems. "Father Tom" got a great kick out of it all and when he watched the little road being ripped up in 1947, he remarked: "There goes my key to hard-to-get lower berths."

Chapter 13

Salamanca and Senecas

Salamanca is the only city in the world on an Indian reservation.

This Southern Tier city of nearly 9,000, a railroad and industrial center, lies almost wholly within the Allegany Reservation which in 1797 was set aside for the Seneca Nation forever.

Salamancans therefore today hold title to their property only by virtue of 99-year leases executed between the city and the Seneca Nation in 1892.

Here is a unique and complex situation. Yet no treaty maker in 1797, before the Iron Horse was born, could foresee the coming of the railroads to the scraggly acres granted the Senecas along the great bend of the Allegheny River. No one in 1797 could know that a corner of that reservation one day the smoke of a booming city would mingle with the haze that hangs eternally over the mountain tops.

Salamanca, named after a Spanish grandee, and a child of the railroads, is one of the youngest communities of the Southern Tier. Until 1863 its site was a swamp. The years since then have been dramatic, struggling years for this young railroad town on the Indian land.

The Allegany Reservation was one of 11 tracts set aside for the Indians at the treaty of Big Tree near Geneseo in 1797. It is a strip of land 40 miles long and a mile wide on either side of the circling Allegheny River. At the time, Joseph Ellicott, the surveyor for the Holland Land Company, declared five-eighths of its 30,000 acres was "inaccessible and untillable lands."

It was Seneca land long before any 1797 treaty—by right of conquest. It was part of the domain which the Nation, in its days of military glory had wrested from the Eries in the fierce warfare of the mid 17th Century. Before the Revolution, the Senecas had a few scattered villages along the Allegheny. After Sullivan's colonial troops during the Revolution devastated the heartland of the Senecas around the Finger Lakes and in the Genesee Valley, some of the defeated tribesmen sought refuge there.

White men came, not with the sword but offering the Bible and the hand of friendship, to live with the Indians in 1798. Three young Quaker missionaries made the first white settlement in what is now Cattaraugus County, in the present town of South Valley. They sought to teach the Indians agriculture and civilized ways. The Society of Friends continued its work on the Reservation for many years.

In 1803 the Quakers bought 609 acres near their first settlement and set up a school for the Indians. They induced the Red Men to start a saw mill in 1812 but after Chief Cornplanter learned that its operation caused friction among his people, he ordered it destroyed, saying "It is better to have peace in our homes than lumber in our houses."

Cornplanter's jurisdiction as sachem of the Nation extended to the Allegany Reservation although he lived over the state line on a tract granted him by the State of Pennsylvania and where his descendants live today. He and other pagan leaders, such as old Governor Blacksnake, opposed efforts of the Quakers to Christianize the reservation Indians.

The Quakers sprang to the aid of the Indians by helping them recover their lands, which the Ogden Land Company

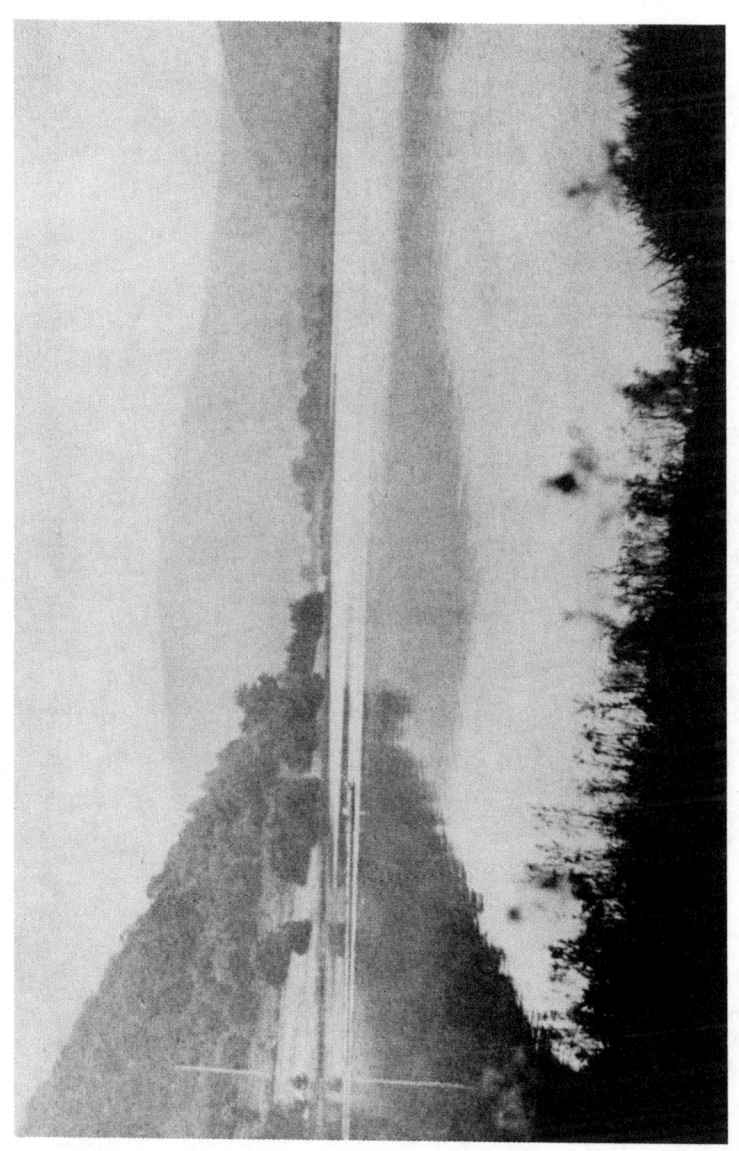

Red House Lake in Allegany State Park

"Garbage Collector" in Allegany State Park

in 1838 had sought to grab by obtaining the signatures of a minority of the chiefs through bribery, firewater and other devious means. The fight was carried to Congress and into the courts before the Indians got clear titles to the Allegany and Cattaraugus Reservations again. They lost much of the Tonawanda Reservation through the Ogden deal.

In 1848 the Indians on the Cattaraugus and Allegany Reservations installed the republic form of government, with elected officers and a council in place of the old rule by chiefs. They hunted and fished on their narrow strip of wild lands along the picturesque river, little disturbed by outside interference.

When the first Erie train came through their lands in 1851, they turned out, some of them in full regalia, to watch in silence the white man's new "smoke devil" puff by. They had signed a treaty nine years before, granting railroads a right of way across their reservation. Otherwise there would be no Salamanca today.

In 1862 another railroad, the Atlantic and Great Western, which later became the Western New York and Pennsylvania and a branch of the Erie, nosed into the Indian domain. It connected with the Erie tracks at a tiny saw mill settlement with the Indian name of Bucktooth. The junction point was renamed Salamanca in honor of Don Jose Salamanca y Mayol, a large stockholder in the road, after the Spanish capitalist had visited the section.

Turntables, shops and engine houses were set up at the erstwhile Bucktooth. When more land was sought for expansion of the rail facilities, the price demanded was so high that the whole installation was moved to an unoccupied and marshy site a mile and half to the eastward. This new center was called East Salamanca until 1873 when it dropped the "East." The onetime Bucktooth became West Salamanca.

From its inception Salamanca was plagued by the land title bogey. Individual leases, negotiated between settlers and the Senecas, were ruled invalid until Congress sanctioned them in 1875.

Then Salamanca grew like the green bay tree. May 16, 1878 was a red letter day for the boom town on the Allegheny. That day the first train over the new Rochester and State Line Railroad, now the Baltimore and Ohio, steamed into town. That day also saw the completion of a pipe line from oil wells in the nearby Town of Carrollton to storage tanks in Salamanca. In 1878 the second brick building in the village, the Opera House, was erected.

Salamanca was on the march, a rapidly growing town with its three railroads, car shops and maze of tracks; with lumber mills and tanneries and oil storage tanks. By 1890 nearly 4,000 people were living where 30 years ago there had been only a swamp. In 1892 Salamanca made a determined but vain attempt to take the county seat away from Little Valley.

A smoky, vital place was Salamanca, as spirited as a young colt, with its railroaders, its lumberjacks and Indians from the reservation giving it life and color. Some lawmakers, barristers and jurymen, in Little Valley for board meetings and court sessions, deserted the more sedate county seat town of nights for its livelier neighbor, the little city by the long river bridge.

Men of Salamanca began making their mark in business and politics. Banker Edward B. Vreeland went to Congress and got into the headlines as the author of a controversial currency act. James S. (Spence) Whipple poured out his eloquence at Republican conventions. In a later day State Senator Albert T. (Ab) Fancher, whose fortune was based on oil and whose finger was in many financial pies, was to command the county GOP for years.

On the Democratic side, Thomas H. Dowd, tall, handsome Irishman who had come to town in the 1880s, a young lawyer from up Humphrey way, rose to prominence in politics and in the court room. He served on the state Supreme Court through appointment by a Democratic governor. Judge Dowd, a venerated figure in Salamanca, closed his law office only a few months before his 94th birthday in the Summer of 1953.

During the years when Salamanca and her citizens were on the march, the shadow of the Indian leases hung over the community. In 1892 the leases were renewed under an agreement whereby the leaseholders were to pay their rent to the Seneca Nation in advance before every February 19.

Some property began to fall in arrears and in 1939 the federal government, as guardian of the Senecas, instituted a test suit to collect back rentals and at the same time demanded a new form of lease with a higher rate of rental. The United States won its case. A Federal Court decision of 1943 broke the back of the Salamanca defense that tender of back rental nullifies any action for recovery, under the state landlord and tenant law. The court held that the state law did not apply on the Indian reservation.

The litigation aroused considerable bitterness. The Indians maintained that they were asking only what was rightfully theirs. But it is only natural that Salamanca people should dislike having to pay the Indians for the mere privilege of living on their land, on top of the regular state and city taxes. They had improved their property, built a city out of a swamp and still do not actually own the land.

But since the litigation of a decade ago, oil has been poured on the troubled waters. The pipe of peace has been smoked along the Allegheny. The lease difficulty was settled, with both sides making compromises. New leases were signed with the higher rental rate. And legislation has been enacted so the state has both civil and criminal jurisdiction over the reservation Indians.

The government also has granted a greater measure of self government to the reservation Senecas. The Indian agency at Salamanca has been closed and the Salamanca lease money is paid directly to the treasurer of the Seneca Nation, instead of to an Indian agent. The city comptroller adds the sum for the lease rental to the other tax bills he sends out and before every Feb. 19 a check for the total amount goes to the Senecas.

The Senecas now also make their own distribution of the cloth guaranteed them annually—four yards per reservation resident—under an ancient treaty. In recent years unbleached muslin has been substituted for the stipulated calico. In 1953 a three-ton shipment of the cloth lay in storage for some months before it was delivered to the Council House for distribution. It seems that because of a shakeup in the Seneca government, there was no official qualified to sign for it.

Few of the 1,100 Indians on the Allegany Reservation till their tax-free land. Many of them have jobs in industry in Salamanca and other centers. Their children go to the Indian School near Red House. Those of the Christian faith attend the Indian Baptist Church and the missionary church on the reservation. In the Council House, where for 150 years the "Peacemakers' Court" of the Indians convened, the colorful religious festivals of the Keepers of the Western Door are held.

Most of the houses along the winding reservation roads are unpainted. On a few there are signs, "Indian baskets and bead work," to catch the tourist trade.

The fortunes of Salamanca, always linked with the railroad car shops, have not been enhanced by the advent of diesel engines. Although some types of diesels are serviced in the Erie shops, it is not as it was in the days of the steam locomotives. The shops of the B. & O. at East Salamanca are quiet, too. But the railroads, the Erie, the B. & O. and the Pennsylvania, are still heavy employers of labor and Salamanca, born of the rails, is still a railroad town.

Other than the railroads, the chief spokes in its economic wheel are its two furniture plants. The largest, the Fancher Company, has added television cabinets to its line. Besides the Fancher plant and that of the Jamestown Table Company, the city has a worsted mill and a plastic molding plant.

Salamanca is looking into the future, not mooning over the past. It currently is embarked on a $1,500,000 public housing project. A Housing Authority, the first in any southwestern New York State community, has been set up to build a 100-dwelling, low-rental housing project near Veterans' Memorial Park. An unusual feature will be a community health clinic. It will house the Salamanca offices of the Cattaraugus County Health Department, which were set up under the Milbank Fund.

Slum clearance is part of the big housing project. A row of old wooden houses in downtown Church Street will be razed to make way for a municipal parking station. Work on the whole project is expected to start early in 1954. Chairman of the Housing Commission is Latham B. Weber, city editor of the *Republican-Press*.

Plans also are under way for a new junior-senior high school near the public housing site. The hiss and smoke of the Iron Horse may have left Salamanca but the spirit of the city is undaunted.

In a little triangular-shaped park along Broad Street stands a boulder over which floats the Stars and Stripes beside an unfamiliar banner. If the visitor stops to investigate, as I did, he will find the second flag is the green and gold banner of the South American republic of Bolivia. And on the boulder in Triangle Park is a tablet stating that it was dedicated in 1941 by the Cattaraugus County American Legion in honor of Simon Bolivar, the Latin-American liberator.

It was put there in recognition of the Spanish origin of the city's name. In 1953 the Bolivian Embassy in Washington sent the flag of the republic, to float beside Old Glory, a symbol of the "Good Neighbor policy."

On the borders of the Indian reservation are two places with curious names. One is Red House, at the gateway to Allegany State Park. It got its name because of a building painted red which in the early days housed raftsmen on the river.

The other oddly-named place is Onoville, just north of the state line. During the lumbering boom it was called Jugville because of the jug of rum that each lumberjack took with him from the tavern there when he went into the woods in the Fall. But residents felt Jugville was undignified, so they called a meeting to pick a new name. At that meeting name after name was proposed. To each one someone would say: "Oh, no, that will never do." A wag spoke up: "Why not call it Onoville?" And Onoville it is to this day.

Part of the Town of Great Valley is within the Allegany Reservation, notably a place with the Indian name of Kill Buck, once the home of an Indian chief of that name.

Two miles north of Great Valley village is a natural phenomenon, the Breathing Well. On the farm now occupied by Lloyd V. Bolles, this well inhales and exhales.

In 1841 Nicholas Flint dug a well 40 feet deep but struck no water. He stoned up the well and covered it over in the vain hope that water might come in during the wet season.

Then he discovered a strong current of air pressing up through the crevices in the platform over the well. He inserted a pump log with a two-inch bore. He found that a current of air was continually blowing out or pressing into the well and that a whistle placed in the bore of the log could be heard half a mile away.

The whistle shrills no more but the old well still "breathes." Farmers say fair or settled weather is indicated when it exhales for a long period; a storm is due when it inhales at length. Scientists explain the phenomenon by the existence of a chain of subterranean caverns connecting with the well and ending in a yet undiscovered outlet. The air currents result from variations in barometric pressure.

* * *

Salamanca is the northern gateway to the largest of all New York State's parks. Allegany State Park's 65,000 acres extend over all or parts of six Cattaraugus County townships and to the Pennsylvania border. It is in the mountains and its highest point is more than 2,300 feet above sea level.

There is nothing artificial about this vast park, except its two lakes. If you crave spectacular scenery and Coney Island-ish excitement, Allegany Park is not for you. But half a million people from all parts of the country who prefer nature in its unspoiled state visit it annually. Some of them start making their cabin reservations in January.

As its manager, Leigh J. Batterson, puts it: "Here the natural forest and wilderness characteristics are combined with modern recreational facilities."

In the forests are sylvan trails, spring-fed brooks, rare flora and fauna. The bear and the deer roam the woods, safe from the hunter's gun. Beavers built their dams in its waters. There are strange geological formations, such as Thunder

Rocks and the Bear Caves, that are reminiscent of Olean's Rock City. A man-made stone observation tower, at an elevation of 2,200 feet, affords a magnificent view, especially when the woods flaunt their Autumnal colors.

The park has 400 cabins, trailer and camp grounds, picnic sites and two swimming pools. Its streams are stocked with fish. In Winter there is skiing, tobogganing and skating. Ski trains run to Salamanca from Buffalo and other cities during the season. There is no hunting in the park—at any season.

The hub of the park is near Red House, where the administration building faces Red House Lake, with its bath house, beach and adjacent athletic fields. Besides the park offices, the administration building houses a museum, full of Indian and pioneer relics, stuffed birds and animals.

The state has owned most of the site of Allegany State Park before. In 1814 the Holland Land Company deeded to New York State all the land between the Allegheny and the Pennsylvania border, with a few tracts excepted. The tract of more than 100,000 acres was called the Donation Lands and was the land company's contribution toward the expense of constructing the Erie Canal.

The state sold the land to speculators and had to take most of it back on tax foreclosure actions. In 1835 Benjamin Chamberlin, an early lumber king, bought the whole expanse. He sold off the land to lumbermen and farmers gradually during the years.

The virgin pine went down and saw mills cut it into shingles and stakes which were rafted down the Allegheny. Several farms were cleared and a few are still operated and privately owned within the area set aside for the state park.

From the Indian days, the area was a mecca of the hunter and the fisherman. One of those who had hunted and fished there for years was Hamilton Ward of Buffalo, state attorney general in 1920. He urged its development as a state park on various naturalist and conservation groups in Buffalo that year and the idea took root.

The movement received the backing of the astute and politically powerful former Senator Fancher of Salamanca. During his lifetime he gave land, money and his time to the state park. It is appropriate that a park pool bears his name today.

Fancher obtained from the economy-minded Republican governor, Nathan L. Miller, an assurance that if $25,000 could be raised by popular subscription, the state would appropriate a like amount for purchase of lands for a park. A fund drive was launched, led by Fancher, Attorney General Ward, Chauncey J. Hamlin, George C. Diehl (three Buffalonians) and Fred G. Kaiser of Dunkirk. They all made liberal contributions. Salamanca raised $5,000, with the present head of the Allegany State Park Commission, Charles E. Congdon, sparking the drive. Buffalo interests chipped in and the required $25,000 was raised. Incidentally, Fred Kaiser is a member of the present commission—as he was of the first in 1921.

That year 7,000 acres were acquired in Quaker Run, near the former Frecks lumber camp and the site of the first white settlement in Cattaraugus County. Allegany State Park was opened on July 30, 1921. It was a modest beginning.

In 1926 the park's share of a fifteen million dollar bond issue for state parks was two-million and large scale purchases of land in the area began. Gradually the park has been developed until today it is the largest scenic public playground in the Empire State.

Cool, inviting woods border nearly all of the 120 miles of roads which wind through its mountainous expanse. Frank Knight, one of the park's nine rangers, an affable and well informed guide, drove us around a great circle of the immense tract. Knight knows every inch of it and is a pal of some of its wild denizens.

We saw several deer in the woods and the ranger stopped the station wagon once and sought to induce his friend, "Lady," to come up to the road. But two small fawn were bounding along in "Lady's" wake and she would not venture out of the woods.

We had hoped to see some of the several friendly black bear that live in the park and that sometimes raid campers' garbage cans in the night. At one point, Knight said: " 'Old Salty' should be along the road around here. That bear is so friendly he will put his head right in my car window, looking for a handout."

But it was not "Old Salty's" day for receiving visitors and we never got a glimpse of him.

Chapter 14

In the "Hills of Home"

In the northeastern corner of Cattaraugus County, in the town of Freedom, among the foothills a little village drowses away the years. Its Yankee settlers gave it the Indian name of Sandusky which means "where there is pure water." But for years and for reasons lost in the mists of time, the place has been called "Henpeck."

"Henpeck" has only two streets, Main and Eagle, and only some 250 people. It was a bigger and busier place before the horseless carriage and the hard roads came to change the whole rural way of life.

I happen to have been born in that village, only one and one half miles from the Wyoming County line so my Southern Tier status might be called "border line." I am not putting my home town in this book purely for sentimental reasons. Sandusky and the Town of Freedom do have some historical interest.

It was on a farm in the Town of Freedom that in 1832, two farmers, digging for coal, made by accident the first subterannean oil strike in New York State. But as one of the prospectors, Wells Cheney, wrote years later: "My partner, Chauncey Spears, was taken suddenly sick and nothing was done until 1864. . . . But I am certain this was the first drop of oil that was ever struck in New York State."

In 1864 an oil company was formed and the next year two test wells were drilled. There was a flow of black lubricating oil but the volume dwindled rapidly and the wells were abandoned. It seems strange that in dairying country, far from the oil fields along the state line, that the first petroleum in the state was struck.

In the Sandusky cemetery is the grave of the last survivor of the Revolution. His name was Daniel Frederick Bakeman and he died on April 5, 1869, at the age of 109 years. Despite other claims, the records show he was the last veteran of the Revolution in America. The DAR placed a marker on his grave in recognition of his distinction. But the last I knew the Bakeman headstone was broken and on the ground —which shouldn't happen in a town with the name of Freedom.

To Freedom and the adjacent towns of Farmersville in Cattaraugus County and Centerville in Allegany in 1841 came the first of a considerable influx of Welsh, thrifty, hearty people with music in their voices. Once the hamlet of Freedom was almost 100 per cent Welsh. About everybody was named Morgan, Jones, Williams, Evans or Owens.

And there are villages whose names bring back memories of my youth when I played baseball in them—Delevan, once Yorkshire Center and renamed for a hotel keeper who trained wrestlers and boxers; Yorkshire, in the old days Yorkshire Corners; Farmersville, Franklinville.

Farmersville's first settlers, in 1816, were three bachelors and one married man. The bachelors drew up a compact which provided that "if any single woman over 14 shall come to reside in our village and no one of this confederacy shall offer her company within a fortnight, the board shall be called together and some one shall be appointed to pay her a visit. Otherwise he must pay a fine sufficiently large to buy the lady a new dress." Farmersville did not long remain a bachelor colony.

At a crossroads between Farmersville and Franklinville stands the old "Checkered Schoolhouse." It has been in national magazines and in Ripley's column. When it was built in 1841, a dispute arose as to whether it should be painted red or white. The "whites" won but one moonlight night the "reds" came to the schoolhouse and covered it with their bright color. A Solomonic trustee, Richard Robins, ended the feud by having the building painted in foot-wide squares, red and white, like a checkerboard.

That pattern was kept until some 50 years ago it was repainted a sober gray. Such an uproar ensued that the old color design was restored. In 1942 the school was closed. Now it is a private residence.

It still bears the sign, "District No. 3, Town of Farmersville, Built in 1841." But its red "checkers" are sadly faded. Is the "checkered schoolhouse" to become only a memory?

Franklinville is the biggest village in the region with a population of more than 2,000. Most of the business places are grouped around its central square with a bandstand in its center. Its principal industry makes television parts.

Franklinville is an old town. Back in 1805 the beauty of the Ischua Valley caught the fancy of a surveyor for the land company, Massachusetts-born Joseph McClure. He bought land and in 1806 built a log cabin in the woods. Around it grew up what was first known only as McClure's Settlement. There was held the meeting at which Cattaraugus County was organized in 1817. McClure, who surveyed many of the early roads of the region, had the faculty of making them converge on his settlement.

In the early days, Franklinville had a "Lazy Society." Any member who performed any avoidable act of physical exercise was haled before a "court." First to be tried were Dr. James Trowbridge, the first physician in the town, and Elijah

Rice. The doctor was charged with unnecessary activity in that he raised a cane to drive a poodle dog from his pantaloons.

Rice's "crime" was that, while seated in a cushioned rocking chair in the shade of his log barn, he held a gun at arms' length and shot a mink which was dragging away one of his hens. He should have waited until his wife brought him another chair on which to rest his gun. Both offenders were fined two gallons of rum, for the consumption of the "Lazy Society."

A modern high school has replaced the old Ten Broeck Free Academy, which was built in 1867 on the four-acre campus and with funds bequeathed by Judge Peter Ten Broeck to provide free education, including the study of astronomy, for the youth of the towns of Franklinville, Farmersville and Machias. Ten Broeck once owned 8,000 acres in the three townships and kept 1,200 head of cattle on his farms, which he personally managed in the plantation manner.

Dutch Hill in the Town of Ischua, Franklinville's southern neighbor, was the scene in 1844–45 of the first and last agrarian revolt in Cattaraugus County history.

"The Dutch Hill War" began in June 1844 when agents of the Holland Land Company sought to evict two brothers, Jacob and George Learn, for defaulting on their land payments. Sheriff George W. White, with a half dozen unarmed aides, started to remove the Learns' effects when they were surrounded by a mob of 150 farmers, some of them armed and some disguised as Indians. The sheriff's men fled but not before White suffered a severe beating.

The incident aroused intense feeling. The rebels held rallies to organize against further eviction attempts.

The "war" was resumed in January, 1845, when three

armed deputies went out from the county seat, Ellicottville, with warrants for the two Learns and two other leaders of the uprising. They found the enemy waiting for them. The forces of the law drew their pistols and got their prisoners. But they encountered a mob on the road back to Ellicottville and were lucky to reach the county seat with one of their prisoners.

Fearing a siege, the sheriff mobilized 800 volunteers to guard the jail and other county buildings. He sent 300 of them out one Sunday to arrest the Learns and other leaders of the revolt. They met no resistance and the Dutch Hill War ended when the land company agreed to let the Learns stay on their premises on condition they keep up their payments and keep the peace.

The county ran up a big bill—for all the mutton hams and other food the defenders of the jail consumed. And the beating Sheriff White got at Dutch Hill is said to have hastened his death.

* * *

Ellicottville's streets are broad and straight and an air of stateliness and consequence clings to this hill-girt village of 1,093, although 85 years have gone since it lost the county seat.

Its square at Washington and Jefferson Streets is the cradle of Cattaraugus. It was there in 1817 that the three commissioners named to pick a site for the new county's seat drove an ironwood post. There later that same year in a frame house were held the first court sessions and the first meeting of the supervisors.

There in 1820 a log prison-court house arose. It burned in 1829 and all the screaming prisoners in the blazing building were saved. In 1830 a brick court house was erected.

It still stands in all its cupaloed dignity, along with its smaller neighbor, the former office of the county clerk. The old county buildings now serve the village's central school system.

In the early days Ellicottville, in the geographical center of the county, was its political, cultural and business center. There was the office of the Holland Land Company and the village took the name of the land agent-surveyor, Joseph Ellicott.

But when the Erie Railroad was built in 1851, it bypassed the shire town. Ellicottville got a railroad, the State Line, in '78, but then it was too late. A rival village to the southwest, Little Valley, on the Erie and with $13,000 and a free site as bait, took away the county seat in 1868. But Ellicottville never lost its air of distinction.

At Washington and Jefferson Streets stands St. John's Episcopal Church, built in 1837, white, exquisite and graceful. In its tower hangs a bronze bell that was cast in Malaga, Spain, in 1708 and for more than a century rang out from a Spanish convent. In 1832 a religious war broke out and the convent was burned. The bell was saved and finally was sold to a New York sea captain as ballast for his ship.

Nicholas Devereux, the land owner whose headquarters were in Ellicottville, bought the bell in New York. He sold it to the village Episcopalians for $125 and in 1838 it came via the Erie Canal to Buffalo, whence it was hauled by horse-team to Ellicottville.

The bell is seven feet in circumference at its base and it weighs 1,300 pounds. On one side is an ornamental cross. Above each arm of the cross is a nail pointing downward at an angle and one on the right side near the bottom. Near its top is a Spanish inscription which is translated as "Hail (I am the voice of the angel who on high sounds forth)

Photo by Mrs. Louise Stuck

Oil Spurts High Over Derrick near Richburg

Wellsville's "Pink House"

Mary full of grace," along with th
Bargas, and the notation, "made at
 Ellicottville was the cradle of St.
told in an earlier chapter. So many
town and moved elsewhere. But the
constant. On one of them is a ski r
trains" from Buffalo and other place

* * *

Life in Little Valley, as in all ru ...., seat towns, quickens when the courts are in session and many feet tread the steps that lead to the Victorian red courthouse with the white trim which rose that proud year of 1868 when Little Valley won the county seat.

The "hub," an old nickname for Little Valley, also is a lively place the first week of every September. That is the traditional date of the County Fair which ran off its 111th edition in 1953.

Across from the courthouse is the domed County Historical Museum, which was dedicated in September of 1911 as a memorial to the soldiers of "the War of the Rebellion." It houses uniforms, firearms and other mementoes of the Civil War, along with Indian and pioneer relics.

The old Rock City Hotel still stands at the familiar crossroads and I wonder if the politicos stage their all-night poker games up in the "Crow's Nest" under its eaves, as they used to years ago. In those years the peppery M. J. Brown, editor of *The Hub,* managed the village ball team and life was real and earnest in the county seat.

Little Valley has its own Rock City. It is not exploited, like the one near Olean, and it is a bit hard to find. On a plateau with an elevation of 2,000 feet, off the Whig Street Road, are 100 acres strewn with huge, strange-shaped boul-

vices between them like streets and with an
 t" in the center.
 e fog-shrouded foothills of Napoli, west of Little Valon December 29, 1951, a C-46 airliner crashed and 26 ersons lost their lives. Fourteen escaped from the wreckage. In early 1953 four St. Bonaventure students were killed when their plane crashed in an isolated section of the town of Lyndon, near Franklinville. Ruggedly beautiful are the hills of old Cattaraugus but death lurks in them for the airmen when storm and fog hide their wooded peaks and slopes.

* * *

Randolph (population 1,455) is a sort of New England picture postcard village, with its many charming white houses testifying to the good taste of its settlers. Many of those settlers came from Randolph, Vt., and named the new community in the pine woods after the old one in the Green Mountains.

It was a college town once—briefly. In 1848 it was the seat of an eclectic college of medicine which shortly merged with a similar one in Syracuse. For half a century Randolph was the site of Chamberlain Institute and its successor, a military school. Now a fine central school stands on the hill which for more than a century has been dedicated to education.

First the Randolph Academy and Female Seminary began life there in 1849. In 1865 Judge Benjamin Chamberlain, a lumbering tycoon, gave $50,000 for a boarding hall on the site on condition that the name of the academy be changed to Chamberlain Institute and that the school trustees be chosen by the Erie Conference of the Methodist Episcopal Church. Chamberlain died before the wooden boarding hall was completed in 1868. His will endowed the Institute with nearly $400,000 but there was long litigation, out of which only $40,000 emerged for the school.

Chamberlain Institute closed its doors in 1904 and the next year Col. James E. Dunn, a West Pointer, a martinet and a flamboyant figure in his "regimentals," leased the property and operated it as military school, drawing students from a wide area, until 1915 when the dormitory burned. It was the third time fire had visited the hill. By that time the grandiose colonel and his school were in the financial mire. There linger in Randolph memories of pitched battles between the military school cadets and the town lads.

Under the Chamberlain will, the Academy assets reverted to the village district, to be used for pupil scholarships. The school borrows from this fund at 4 per cent and loans the money to the scholarship pupils. So annually the school board holds two sessions. First it meets as the Central School board. Then it adjourns and reconvenes as the trustees of Randolph Academy.

Midway between Randolph and its smaller sister, East Randolph, is the Western New York Home for Homeless and Dependent Children. It was established by the Rev. Charles Strong, a former chaplain at Sing Sing Prison, in 1877 when he took in three waifs. A society was organized and an endowment set up. Among the early supporters was Governor Fenton. The home now houses about 100 children from several Western New York counties. Some of them are committed by the juvenile courts to the wholesome envoronment of the home-like place in the Southwestern Cattaraugus hills.

Randolph's industries include a furniture factory, a tin can plant and machine shop of the Borden milk combine and a metallic ladder factory, which recently made the aluminum scaffolding used for cleaning the lofty chamber of the United States Supreme Court. It can be tucked away, out of sight like a folding bed, during the sessions of the august nine.

The village also is the site of a state fish hatchery, in whose cold spring waters are hatched the brown trout eggs for the other hatcheries of the state.

In the early 1890s a native found what he thought was gold on Pine Hill in the Town of Elko. Analysis showed his find was not gold but a rotten stone ore which was suitable for making paint. The Elko Mining Company was formed with headquarters in Randolph and it produced paint for several years.

This town also produced some interesting people. One was Dr. Frederick Larkin who held a degree in medicine but chose to operate a jewelry store, build houses and deal in real estate, while achieving renown on the side as an archeologist and anthropologist, with rather unorthodox religious views.

Joel H. Foy, who made a fortune in the pharmaceutical business, got his start in a Randolph drug store. He joined forces with Bert Maltbie, a drug clerk in the village, who conceived a formula for combining drugs in pill form, rather than in the then standard powders prescribed by physicians. Out of that grew the big Maltbie Chemical Company of New Jersey. Foy gave the Randolph Free Library as a memorial to his wife a $50,000 building and a $30,000 endowment fund, with the stipulation the village help support the library through a two-mill tax levy.

A onetime editor of the now 90-year-old *Randolph Register* was the fabulous "King James" Strang. While in Randolph he claimed he could "handle serpents, heal the sick, cast out devils and eat deadly poison." The village scientist, Doctor Larkin, challenged him at a gathering to eat some strychnine tablets, enough to kill ten men. Strang ducked the issue by dismissing his audience as "unbelievers."

He left Randolph and became a leader in the Mormon church. In 1849 he broke with Brigham Young, the new head of the church, and founded a colony of his own on Beaver Island off the Michigan coast. There he built a castle and a tabernacle and had himself crowned "king" of 1,200 subjects.

King James took unto himself seven wives. His original spouse departed. Then he issued a ukase that all women of the colony wear bloomers, a practice he had advocated in Randolph. All but one of the women obeyed and Strang had that woman's husband, John Bedford, flogged in public.

The vengeful Bedford and another man fled to Mackinac City, where they boarded a vessel sent out by the United States government to investigate charges that the Strangites preyed on lake commerce. The story is that Bedford shot King James from the deck of that ship. He was tried for murder and acquitted. The wounded monarch asked to be taken to the Wisconsin home of his first wife and there he died after 11 days. His tabernacle was burned and his kingdom vanished.

* * *

The village of Cattaraugus (population 1,190 and elevation 1,383 feet) came into being with the Erie Railroad in 1851. Joseph Plumb, who owned most of the village site, was appalled by the rough and lawless ways incident to the building of a railroad and when he sold his lots, each deed carried a proviso that no intoxicants were to be sold on the property.

One buyer named Tubbs began selling spirits in the building he had erected on his lot. Plumb took legal possession of the property under the terms of the deed. Tubbs carried the test case to the State Court of Appeals and lost. Whereupon Plumb restored the property to the Tubbs family.

Under his will Plumb sought to make the restrictions against the sale or manufacture of intoxicants on his onetime property binding for all time. Today the words, "subject to the Plumb restrictions" are inserted in every deed. The temperance zealot also decreed that all forfeited properties were to go to the Congregational Church of Otto.

In the 1930s the local WCTU sought to prevent the granting of a beer license to a village hotel, but the remaining Plumb heirs were not interested in the issue and the Otto church had been absorbed into a federated body. So the hotel got its license. One wonders if the spirit of Joseph Plumb, foe of the demon rum and dead these 83 years, does come back once in a while to haunt that barroom on his "restricted" land.

* * *

Cattaraugus Creek, which forms the northern boundary of its namesake county, cuts the village of Gowanda in twain.

The southern part, in the Town of Persia, Cattaraugus County, has 2,221 inhabitants and most of the business places. Divided Gowanda is the largest village in Cattaraugus County. The northern sector, in the Town of Collins, Erie County, has a population of 1,088. The village government disregards the county line.

Gowanda was first called Lodi and it was in the office of the *Lodi Messenger* that a tramp printer named Horace Greeley obtained work for six months in 1830. In 1848 the village was renamed Gowanda, an Indian word meaning "under the cliffs." The name is apt. Along the Cattaraugus in the vicinity are some noble cliffs.

Gowanda is a substantial sort of community, going its brisk way without undue blast of trumpets. It is the site of the largest glue factory in the world, that of the Peter Cooper Company, and of a large tannery, the Moench Company, which is a subsidiary of the Brown Shoe Company. Both of these industries are on the Cattaraugus side of the creek—and in the Southern Tier.

East and south of Gowanda along the Cattaraugus stretches the scenic Zoar Valley, with its fertile bottom lands where grapes and berries grow, its steep green hillsides, its farms, Summer homes, cabins and camps. Long ago Buffalo people who like nature "discovered" the Valley of Zoar. In that valley is a large natural gas storage field. The gas was there when the Indians named the stream "foul-smelling banks."

In 1810 the first white settler, Ahaz Allen, came down the Cattaraugus in a canoe and beheld that beautiful valley. Reminded of the Biblical city of plains from which Lot fled, he gave it the name of Zoar.

In the far northwestern corner of the county is the village of Perrysburg, since 1912 the site of the J. N. Adam Memorial Hospital, established by the city of Buffalo for the treatment of tuberculosis. Bearded merchant Adam, then mayor of Buffalo, gave the 300 acres on which the hospital buildings stand, on a hill south of the village and 1,450 feet above sea level and commanding a grand view of Lake Erie and much of two counties.

The northwestern corner of Cattaraugus County also embraces a small slice of Indian land, part of the Cattaraugus Indian Reservation, nearly all of which lies in Erie County. The Senecas who live there act in concert with their brethren of the Allegany Reservation with whom they are joined in the Seneca Republic.

The Cattaraugus Reservation is better land than the Allegany Reserve but again few reservation Indians till the soil. Most of them work in industry in nearby communities. Some work in the vast berry patches or in the canneries of the region.

Through the Indian land the Cattaraugus winds its way to join Lake Erie in the county of Chautauqua. All are those place names are of Indian origin.

Chapter 15

Allegany, "Roof of the Tier"

Allegany County is named after an old Indian river which is spelled "Allegheny" and which does not cross one inch of its soil.

It is the smallest of the four western counties of the Southern Tier in area (1,048 square miles) and in population (43,000). It also is the highest. The "roof" of the Southern Tier reaches its apex in Alma Hill in southern Allegany County, 2,548 feet above the level of the sea. The length and breadth of old Allegany, the hills stand guard, scalloped against the sky, all the way from Centerville to Ceres, from Short Tract to Shongo.

Even from the highest peaks come bumper crops, particularly of potatoes and milk, as well as from the rich bottom lands of the Genesee, the northward flowing river which winds through the length of the county.

In this rugged land is the spring known to the Indians long before the palefaces came, the spring whose oil-laden waters inspired the first record of petroleum in America. The first test well in New York State was driven deep into Allegany earth. For three quarters of a century its buckled terrain has been yielding its liquid treasure and Allegany leads the counties of the Empire State in the production of oil and natural gas.

Allegany's thick woods and quiet hills are the delight of the deer hunter. There are great white spaces on Allegany's map. Back in the hills are roads so remote that any passing automobile, other than that of the rural mail carrier, is an event. Paradoxically this same county is the only one in the western part of the Tier to boast two centers of higher education. Its first settler, in a lonely forest cabin, was a graduate of Yale.

This is old Indian country. Along the Genesee stood the southernmost village of the Senecas. At Caneadea "Castle" the war parties gathered, the chiefs held their ceremonious councils and white prisoners ran the gauntlet.

After the Indians lost their homeland, the land came into the hands of the white speculators, the western portion belonging to the Holland Land Company, the eastern to Phelps and Gorham, with Robert Morris reserving a southern chunk and Philip Church owning a large tract in the center.

Many of the pioneers came into the new country with only a gun, an axe and a few dollars to pay down on their lands. Grimly they took up the task of conquering the formidable hills that isolated them, of clearing the dark pine forests, of battling the stony soil, the fierce Winters and the awful loneliness.

It was in the 1850s that the whistle of the Erie steam cars and the horn of the Genesee Valley boatmen brought the better time to the county that had been carved out of the backwoods in 1806.

More than most counties, Allegany has retained the rugged characteristics of the pioneers. For one thing, it has no industrial cities. It has only one community, the bustling oil-rich village of Wellsville, of more than 5,000 people. It mostly gets its living from the soil—and that includes its mineral resources.

People *live* in Allegany's hills. This is not Summer resort country. Many of Allegany's people live on the same acres their fathers did. Four out of five of them vote the Republican ticket their fathers did. Mostly they are of the old stock —Yankees, eastern Yorkers, Pennsylvanians and the Germans and the Irish who long ago came to the foothills to escape the tyrannies of the Old World.

They don't like directives, whether they come from Washington on the Potomac or Belmont on the Genesee. They stand on their own two feet. The chances are those two feet will be planted firmly on the slope of a steep hill—and pointed toward the peak.

Chapter 16

River-Canal Towns

Once upon a time a half dozen Northern Allegany communities were doubly blessed. They not only were on a river—the Genesee—but they also were on a canal—the Genesee Valley.

Seventy-five years have gone by since a boatman's horn has echoed in the ports of Fillmore, Houghton, Caneadea, Oramel and Belfast. The Genesee Valley Canal served that region for less than 30 years but they were colorful, remembered years. And the old ditch made some of those towns.

Canals may come and canals may go but a river goes on forever. The northward flowing Genesee is shallow—except in flood time—and it never was a navigable stream. But the mere presence of a river in its midst gives something to a town, an intangible something that is in the realm of the spirit. Those who live on a river will know what I mean.

Most northerly of the river villages in Northern Allegany that once were canal ports is Fillmore. It began as a tiny settlement where Cold Creek joins the Genesee and it was called "Mouth of the Creek." In 1850 the Genesee Valley Canal came and the place began to boom. The postoffice established that year at the mouth of the creek was named Fillmore after the Buffalo lawyer-politico who sat in the White House.

In 1950 the village celebrated its centennial. The men grew beards and they and their womenfolk dug oldtime costumes out of attic trunks. That is the accepted pattern for centennials these days.

But Fillmore evolved something new for its birthday party. Instead of the trite "Century of Progress" slogan, Fillmore publicized its centennial as "A Century of Rigor Mortis." The unusual slogan attracted national attention. The major press services carried the story. There was a paragraph about Fillmore's centennial in *Time* magazine.

Fillmore is not by no means a dead town. It is the liveliest community in Northern Allegany, with a population of more than 500 and it is the trading center for a wide area. But its business section is not prepossessing. Many of the business places are of frame, one story, and with false fronts. Centennial promoters admitted the main street looked like "a frontier movie set."

The unique centennial slogan had a two-fold purpose. One was to get publicity—and the promoters got it beyond their wildest dreams. The other was the hope that it would bring an improvement in the appearance of Main Street buildings.

It did. The postoffice and other buildings have been modernized and given new fronts. Fillmore no longer looks so much like a "frontier movie set."

Hume, an older village in the hills only a mile northwest of Fillmore, was the important center before the canal came. Now it might almost be called a suburb of Fillmore. Huge crops of potatoes are raised around Hume and in the Wyoming towns of Bliss and Pike.

George Harding has been dead for 20 years but his name is still a legend in the hill country. The Hume lawyer had a flashing wit and a flair for the biting phrase. He was a master of court room strategy.

Harding cared not a fig for the conventions. In Winter he

pinned up his overcoat with a huge horse-blanket pin. He chewed tobacco incessantly and his spitting precision was remarkable. He would remove his shoes in the court room, even when appearing before the august Appellate Division. He was a short man, slightly built, and he feared neither judge, rival barrister, man or devil. Once he upset a rather stuffy dinner of a bar society in the Olean House by bellowing: "Where is the water closet?"

Whenever he tried a case or presided over one, for he also was a peace justice, crowds flocked from all over the countryside. And he always gave them a show.

Once a judge fined Harding $5 for contempt of court. The lawyer had spoken most disrespectfully of the jurist. Harding forked over a $10 bill. "I said $5, Lawyer Harding," said the judge. "Keep it," retorted Harding. "I shall probably utter another $5 worth of contempt before this case is over."

Again when another jurist slapped a $5 fine on Harding for contempt, the Hume lawyer merely said: "I will apply it on account." It seemed the judge owed him money.

* * *

There was no rougher port on the old Genesee Valley Canal than Houghton. It was known as "Jockey Street," because of the Sunday horse races staged there. There were many brawls and much carousing in the village tavern.

Today Houghton is a serene and immaculate college town, probably the only one in the East in which neither tobacco nor alcoholics are sold. On a hill overlooking the village and the river is the campus of Houghton College, a citadel of the Wesleyan Methodist Church.

It was founded in 1883 as Houghton Wesleyan Methodist Seminary. A moving spirit in its pre-natal period was Willard J. Houghton, a descendant of the pioneers after whom the village was named. His childhood home was on the site of the campus that bears his name today.

Willard Houghton was a devout man, strong in the Wesleyan faith. He was distressed by the sinful goings-on in "Jockey Street." He organized a Sunday School and traveled around the countryside, scattering Bible picture cards for the youngsters and tracts for their elders. He became an itinerant Wesleyan Methodist preacher and took part in the first conference that led to the founding of Houghton Seminary.

Leaders of the church decided on the rural village as an ideal site for a denominational school because "it was free from the evils of the larger towns and cities." Houghton took up the first collection for the new seminary in the little white church, which, shorn of its steeple, is now used as a recreation building for the college.

After a struggle to raise the needed funds, Houghton Seminary was opened in 1884 on "Old Sem Hill," about a quarter of a mile south of the village limits. It outgrew that campus and moved to its present site in 1905.

In the seminary's second graduating class was a farm youth from nearby Short Tract. His name was James Seymour Luckey and his name is a venerated one at Houghton College. He did janitor work in his seminary days to defray his expenses. He went on to Oberlin and to Harvard and in 1908 returned to Houghton as president of the school where he had been a janitor. Houghton was chartered as a college in 1923.

Doctor Luckey headed the college until his death in 1937, when the then 28-year-old dean and the present president, Dr. Stephen W. Paine, took the helm.

Houghton College had an enrollment of 625 students, 322

men and 333 women, for the 1952–53 term. Among them are many with musical talent and the college's musical groups, particularly its a-capella choir, are widely known. The college has grown rapidly in recent years, with three major buildings added to its plant.

On its scenic campus a bit of the Indian lore of the Genesee Valley is preserved in the form of a huge granite boulder. It marks the last resting place of Copperhead, the last Seneca Indian living in the Town of Caneadea. He died in 1864 and he claimed he was 120 years old.

The inn that had been the center of iniquity in the days of the canal boats and the Sunday horse races still stands, moved back from the highway and remodeled into the home of Prof. Charles Finney, chairman of the college music division.

In the college catalog under the heading "Standards of Conduct," is this significant paragraph: "The college is opposed to practices which lead to the wasting of time under questionable circumstances, such as card playing, dancing and attendance at theaters; or which tend to the weakening of body and mind, such as the use of tobacco and alcoholic liquors."

That is why the one time Jockey Street, the wickedest place on the Valley Canal, today is a college town in which neither tobacco nor alcoholic liquors are on sale.

* * *

The Indians had an important town in the river valley long before the white men built their settlements and dug their canal there. Caneadea, a village of 30 log huts, southernmost town of the Seneca nation, stood on the east bank of the Genesee, opposite Houghton's hilltop campus. Caneadea means in the Indian tongue, "where the heavens rest upon the earth."

It was at that Seneca village that Mary Jemison, the fabulous "White Woman of the Genesee," stopped to rest on her long journey from the Ohio River to her new home up the Valley. She had walked 300 miles, her papoose strapped upon her back. The white girl who had been taken captive by the Indians lived the rest of her long life in the Indian way.

British soldiers came to Caneadea during the Revolution to build a log council house beside the river as a gesture of good will toward their Seneca allies. That council house resounded to the oratory of Red Jacket and Cornplanter. From its doors went out the red warriors to raid frontier settlements. With them went the Genesee chiefs, Little Beard, Tall Chief, Half Town and John Hudson, the head man at Caneadea town. There was a white man in the ranks, Captain Nellis, the renegade who lived at Caneadea with his Indian wife and half-breed children.

It was to Caneadea during the Revolution that the Senecas brought Moses Van Campen, the border scout, the Daniel Boone of Allegany, a prisoner. It was there he ran the gauntlet, 30 yards from the trail to the Council House, through a line of women, armed with clubs and whips. Van Campen ducked and dodged his way, almost unscathed, to within a few feet of sanctuary. In his path were only two young squaws with whips poised to strike the bare back of the captive. Van Campen sent one sprawling with a football straight arm. He kicked the other in the stomach and she joined her comrade on the ground. The braves guffawed. Moses Van Campen became a venerated figure in Allegany County. He led parades and was on the platform at pioneer celebrations. None paid him greater respect than the Indians.

After the Revolution, at the treaty of Big Tree in 1797, the Senecas were allotted 10,000 acres around their old village of Caneadea. In 1826 they sold their reservation and most of them moved away. But some remained in the neighborhood and settlers got to know characters with such picturesque names as John Shanks, Long Beard and Copperhead.

The white men took the old Indian name of Caneadea for the village they built on the west side of the river, two miles northeast of the old Seneca town.

The Senecas abandoned their council house, along with their reservation. A pioneer, Joel Seaton, bought the land where it stood and moved the building nearer the road that had been an Indian trail. He used it as a dwelling for a time. Then the historic house fell into disuse and decay and for many a year it stood along the river road, forlorn and neglected.

In 1870 William Pryor Letchworth, the public-spirited Buffalonian who later gave his beautiful estate, Glen Iris, at the falls of Portage, to the state for the park which now bears his name, had the historic Council House moved from Caneadea to Glen Iris. There, amid the scenic splendor of "The Grand Canyon of the East," at Letchworth State Park, it stands today—near the monument at the grave of "The White Woman."

There's an historical marker along the Genesee to tell the place where the Council House and the Indian village stood.

Midway between the villages of Caneadea, in the river valley, and Rushford, amid the hills, the Rochester Gas and Electric Corporation in 1926–27 built a huge power dam. The dam holds the water of a large artificial lake of considerable scenic charm. This lake covers the onetime hamlet of East Rushford and many farm acres. It has been stocked with fish and there are many cottages on its shores.

When it came to naming the project, Caneadea and Rushford collided headon. Each wanted the lake and dam to bear its name. Caneadeans put up a sign: "Caneadea Lake and Dam." Rushfordites tore it down and substituted one that read: "Rushford Lake and Dam." After months of such feuding a compromise was reached—Caneadea Dam and Rushford Lake.

Yankees settled Rushford and the quiet village amid the hills has retained its New Englandish flavor. It has more charming, well-kept, old fashioned white houses with green blinds and fan windows than any other village of its size in the Southern Tier.

In one of the old white houses, a governor of the state, Frank Higgins, was born. In that same house the well-known writer, Philip Wylie, spends his Summers. You hardly expect to find one of America's most sophisticated writing men in an out-of-the-way village. He married the daughter of the owner of the white house, widow of a village physician. In Rushford he is not the noted author of "Generation of Vipers," and other rather iconoclastic works. He is Jennie Ballard's son-in-law and that is the way he wants it.

Rushford is many miles from the present oil fields but it was in that township in July, 1861, that the first recorded test well for petroleum in New York State was completed. Early settlers long had skimmed the oil off two springs on the John Moore farm for boot and harness grease. The well did not yield oil in paying quantities and it was abandoned after several attempts.

* * *

At Belfast the old canal swung away from the river and cut across the rugged hills southwest to Cuba and to Olean. Belfast began life in 1824 as Orrinsburgh. The great Genesee flood of 1836 washed the little settlement away. The pioneers built anew, on higher ground, and they called the new place, Belfast, after an older town on the Irish sea.

Because of two fighting Irishmen, the eyes of the sporting world were fixed for a few months in 1889 on the river village. For there Billy Muldoon, onetime wrestling champion of the world, was training John L. Sullivan, for the July 2 bout in which he was to defend his heavyweight boxing title against Jake Kilrain.

It was not by chance that the farming community in the foothills was chosen for the training camp. Billy Muldoon had been born in those hills. Some years before, he had built in Belfast village a house with roomy porches on all sides. There were other buildings, a training stable, a carriage house, servants' quarters, a horse barn and eventually a bowling alley.

John L., an irresponsible playboy, had come to Belfast "a drunken mass of flesh and bone," to quote Muldoon. In two months the iron-willed, tyrannical Muldoon had whipped the Boston Strong Boy back into shape—so that he conquered Kilrain at Richburg, Miss., after 75 rounds and two hours and 18 minutes of bare knuckle, toe-to-toe fighting.

It had been no easy task. Muldoon put Sullivan through the most rigorous training routine any champion ever knew. And he hardly let the dram-loving John L. out of his sight. But sometimes the champ would elude his jailer. Then, they will tell you down the river, the cry would go up in the streets of Belfast:

"John L. is loose again. Send for Muldoon."

And Muldoon would come, snatch the champ away from the bar, toss him into the back of a buckboard and cart him back to camp.

Muldoon maintained his Belfast training camp until 1892. Then "the Iron Duke" founded his famous health center near White Plains. He gave his Belfast property to the Catholic church. The house where John L. slept was used for a time as a convent. Now it is a private home, shorn of most of its wide porches. A onetime training stable still stands. From its ceiling hangs two iron rings on which once the great John L. Sullivan swung.

Many people will remember Belfast as the village by the "long bridge." The Genesee Viaduct which carries the freight trains of the Erie cutoff over the valley just north of Belfast is 3,119 feet long and 141 feet high. It is undoubtedly one of the longest railroad bridges in the state. Two miles east of Fillmore is another Erie cutoff viaduct which is higher (155 feet) but shorter (1,922 feet in length) than the great span near Belfast. Both bridges represent an engineering triumph of 1910.

Chapter 17

Philip Church's Old Domain

Angelica has less than 1,000 inhabitants and it is not a particularly busy place these days. But about the serene old village with the melodious name clings an aura of departed glory.

There are remnants of its past consequence—the broad principal street, the public square, ringed by four churches, the ancient court house and gracious old homes. All these things tell the visitor, even after 150 years, that long ago someone planned great things for Angelica.

That someone was Philip Church, the father of Allegany County and the owner of 100,000 wildwood acres. He picked the center of that tract for its capital and he gave the village he founded there his mother's name, Angelica.

When Allegany County was formed in 1806, its whole territory was the town of Angelica. And Philip Church saw to it that the village of that name was made the shire town, even if it involved taking three townships from Steuben so that Angelica would be the geographical center of the new county.

Judge Church gave the public square to Angelica "for all time" and he donated the land for the four churches. He opened a land office to attract settlers and among those who came were distinguished French exiles. He built a store, a saw mill and roads to his village. He chose a site nearby for his own mansion and 2,000 acre estate. He made Angelica the most important center in Allegany County in the pioneering time.

He was instrumental in bringing the Erie Railroad and the Genesee Valley Canal to the region but both bypassed Angelica. And it was Angelica's lack of a railroad that lost it the county seat to Belmont.

Fortune has not been kind to the "mother of Allegany." Angelica finally got a railroad, around the turn of the century, when the Shawmut was built over the great ridges of the Southern Tier and of Northern Pennsylvania. It got the Shawmut car shops, too, largely because the president of the road, Frank Sullivan Smith, lived in the village, in a big ornate house. But Smith died and so, in time, did the Shawmut and the car shops.

Angelica fought hard to remain the shire town. In 1858 the county seat was moved to Belmont which was on the Erie Railroad and new county buildings rose in the Genesee River village. But Angelica did not give up and from 1860 to 1892 alternate court terms were held in the two villages, only seven miles apart.

About all Angelica has been able to retain of its oldtime prestige is the site of the county fair and the county home. Since 1843 the Allegany County Fair has held forth in the village.

Still standing, at a bend of the Genesee some two miles southwest of Angelica, is the stately manor house Philip Church completed in the year of 1810. Long ago it passed out of the hands of the Churches but it still keeps the name Philip Church gave it—Belvidere.

According to tradition, he picked its site by shinnying up a tall pine tree in the virgin forest and sighting out the land. That was in 1800 and on his first visit to the Genesee Country. He had come from New York to Canandaigua, the capital of the frontier, to bid in at foreclosure sale the 100,000 acres which Robert Morris, the land speculator, had put up as security for the $80,000 loan he had obtained from Philip's father, John Barker Church.

John Barker Church, a well-born Englishman, had come to America to seek his fortune under the assumed name of John Carter. He espoused the cause of American independence and was a commissary-general to the French army in America. He became a friend of Washington and Lafayette.

John B. Church allied himself to a wealthy and powerful colonial family by marrying the lovely Angelica, daughter of General Philip Schuyler. Another daughter married Alexander Hamilton. In 1778 a son was born to the Churches and he was named Philip after grandfather Schuyler.

After the Revolution, the family lived in England for a time and young Philip grew up in a cultured and aristocratic atmosphere. He attended Eton College, studied in London's Middle Temple and hobnobbed with the great and the near great.

After the family returned to America to live, young Philip served on the staff of George Washington and as private secretary to his uncle, the celebrated Hamilton. He remembered filing away among other papers the final draft of Washington's farewell address.

Originally the estate along the Genesee was planned as a summer home for Philip's parents. But John B. Church spent only one summer there. His tangled affairs called him back to New York and to England.

In 1804 Philip Church built a temporary home in the wilds. It was a two-story frame house, the first painted building in the state west of Canandaigua. It was called "The White House" and it stood until 1902 when a gale ripped it down.

It was to that home that in 1805 Philip brought his bride, the 19-year-old socialite, Anna Matilda Stewart of Philadelphia, whom he had met while attending the funeral of George Washington. Their wedding journey was a strange one, first by coach and four to Bath, then by jolting wagon to Hornellsville, whence they rode on horseback along a blazed trail in the forest. When they reached the White House, the pack horses with bedding and provisions were far behind, so they slept that night on straw, harried by howling wolves outside and prowling rats inside.

Work began on the manor house in 1807. It was finished in 1810. The eminent Benjamin Latrobe was its architect and neither pains nor expense were spared in its building. Its brick and stone and its hand-hewn timbers came from the Church lands but the workmen were imported from the East.

Today it stands as a tribute to the good taste of an early generation—two stories of noble brick and stone, its Ionic pillars facing the curving Genesee. It sets well back from the road behind a low wall of stone and high walls of trees and shrubbery. The long one-story brick wing on the east was added about 1814, in the fashion of English country houses. Belvidere has 26 high-ceilinged rooms with many floor-deep windows and with 13 fireplaces.

In that home Philip Church's young bride, so suddenly transplanted from the sophisticated whirl of Philadelphia society to a primitive life on a wild frontier, easily adjusted herself to her new environment. She made friends with the Indians who called her Ye-nun-ke-awa, which means "first white woman." In 1812 when her husband was stranded abroad because of the War with Britain, the Indians, who knew a battle was raging at Fort Erie, camped at Belvidere for two days to protect Mrs. Church and the children.

Through the years Philip Church, chosen in 1809 the first judge of Allegany County, sold his lands, developed his estate, guided the affairs of his community and of his nine children and lived the life of a country gentleman. Notable guests came to Belvidere—the Schuylers and the Rensselaers and other kinfolk; Thomas Morris, son of Robert; Robert Troup, the land agent; Horatio Seymour, once a candidate for President, the Wadsworths from their estates in the Middle Genesee Valley.

Judge Church was deeply interested in agriculture and once brought from Albany in his gig a crated Spanish Merino sheep, the first of that breed in Western New York. He died in 1861, full of years and of honors, and sleeps in Angelica's old "Until the Dawn" cemetery.

After him, his son, Richard, a genial squire with little talent for business, lived on the estate. In 1892, beset by financial difficulties, he sold Belvidere.

During the occupancy of the Churches, the mansion housed many treasures, among them the private papers of Hamilton and the pistols he carried to his death in his duel with Aaron Burr. They had belonged to John B. Church, who had used them in a bloodless duel with the same Burr. Later Philip Church loaned them to Hamilton's son, Philip, who was mortally wounded in a duel. Now the historic pistols are the property of the Bank of the Manhattan Company in New York, a bank founded by Aaron Burr.

It was at Belvidere, according to tradition, that the baggage check was born. William Morris, grandson of Robert Morris, was an official of the Erie Railroad and while visiting Richard Church, hit upon the idea of numbering pasteboard pieces. Loss of bagage was heavy on the railroad. Church suggested the brass and leather straps to tie the pieces together.

Just before its purchase by the present owner, Robert B. Bromeley, Bradford, Pa., newspaper and radio station owner, in 1947, Belvidere was neglected and forlorn. The previous owner, S. Hoxie Clark, had died and the whole estate bore an unkempt look. The fate of a distinguished homestead hung in the balance.

Now an old and gracious way of life has come back to Belvidere. The Bromeleys have restored it to its oldtime dignity and immaculate grooming.

The coming of the French families to Angelica in 1805–06, added a sophisticated tone to the raw settlement on the frontier. Early among the new arrivals were Madame d'Autremont and her sons, Alexander and Augustus. They had fled France at the outbreak of the Revolution in that country and with other Royalists had found refuge at the short-lived settlement near Towanda, Pa., on the Susquehanna, established by Talleyrand and called Asylum. The d'Autremonts were pioneer tavern keepers and merchants in Angelica and their descendants still live in the region.

Angelica was briefly a haven for another French exile, a famous one in his time, the Baron Hyde de Neuville. After the restoration of the monarchy, he returned to France and became that nation's minister to the United States. His wife was an artist and in 1807 she painted the main street of Angelica—a huddle of houses amid stumps and with cattle grazing along the road, not an enchanting scene.

Another Frenchman, not a titled one but bearing a family name that was to become famous in America, lived for three years in Angelica. Victor du Pont de Nemours came, not to find a haven, but to make money. He had preceded his father and older brother, Eleuthere Irenee, to America and had been in the French diplomatic service. His brother founded the great du Pont industrial dynasty in Delaware on the banks of the Brandywine in 1802. Victor was of help in that enterprise because of his knowledge of American customs. But he chose to go in for land speculation rather than the making of gunpowder.

The Spring of 1806 found him in Angelica where he bought 500 acres of uncleared land of Philip Church. His name appears on the first deed recorded in Allegany County. He opened a little store on Main Street at the square and in the Fall, after clearing 10 acres, he went to Delaware for his family. He bought a house on South Street on his return. For two years all went well. The farm prospered. Du Pont became active in community affairs, as a major of the militia, as a "roadmaster" and a school trustee. He was Angelica's first town clerk and in 1808 was elected Allegany's second county clerk.

But the store steadily lost money and du Pont found himself in financial straits. Added to his troubles was a bitter political quarrel with Judge Church. Finally, in the Fall of 1809, Victor du Pont de Nemours yielded to the pleas of his brother to return to Delaware and with his family he left the Genesee Country forever—after making an assignment for the benefit of his creditors.

The cream-colored brick former court house that still stands on the square in Angelica was built in 1819. It now serves as a community building. It is saturated with history.

The old court house, some contend, is the cradle of the Republican Party. It was there in October, 1854, that a dozen Whigs and some 50 Free Soil Democrats met for the first Republican convention in New York State—and it is claimed, first in the nation. It nominated Myron H. Clark for governor. Ripon, Wis., vigorously disputes Angelica's claim and seemingly with good reason. A similar Republican state convention met in Ripon in the Spring of 1854. Angelica's neighbor, Friendship, also claims the honor because a convention was called there earlier that same year—but nobody attended except the promoters.

One Spring day in 1824 Angelica was jammed with people, 10,000 of them from all over the countryside, among them 50 Indians from the Caneadea Reservation. They had come for a spectacle—to see David How hanged in the public square for the murder of Othello Church, the first execution in Allegany County.

Feeling ran high. Some felt the slaying had been justified. How claimed Church, a prosperous Friendship miller, and six other men had ruined him financially, had even seized his crops. He called them "the seven devils." He said when he asked them to leave enough grain to feed his family during the Winter, they not only refused but tore up the vegetables in his garden. Church was asked to leave some onions and for answer spat in How's face.

A few nights later the mill and barns of one of the seven, John Palmer, was burned. How was arrested for arson but discharged for lack of evidence. Still he brooded over his wrongs and sought further revenge. Early one December morning Othello Church answered a knock at the door of his kitchen. He opened the door and received a fatal bullet in his chest. How later confessed the murder.

When the time came to hang David How in the public square, he was escorted from the jail to the gallows by the sheriff on horseback and a hollow square of the militia. Sheriff Wilson's face was white and drawn. He nearly fainted as he pulled the rope. To the last he feared a bullet from the crowd. For he was one of the "seven devils" who had hounded How.

* * *

Belmont lays no claim to Angelica's wealth of history. It bows to the greater antiquity of its neighbor to the north. Belmont can afford to be magnanimous. After all is it not Belmont that has the county seat, undisputed these 61 years?

Belmont is the capital of the Town of Amity (a pleasing name), as well as of the County of Allegany. Settlement began in the township as early as 1803 but it was not until 1833 that the village that in its earlier days was variously Philipsville and Philipsburgh (both names honored Philip Church) really began to sprout.

That was the year Judge Church and four other men, all of them new arrivals from Washington County, bought and began to develop the Philipsburgh Mill Reserve. It was the water power of the Genesee that spawned the enterprise. A village was laid out and the high plateau above the river, "The Table Knoll," was designated as the site of the public buildings. It is there the modern county building, erected in 1938, perches today.

The coming of the Erie Railroad and the consequent removal of the county seat from Angelica boomed the village whose name was changed to Belmont, suggested by a distinguished resident, Hamilton Ward, Sr.

This county seat town on the Genesee is a pleasant village in a broad and fertile valley, with its big milk plant in the heart of a dairying section and on the fringe of the oil country.

Chapter 18

Named for a Saxon King

It is 3 o'clock of a Sunday afternoon in midsummer and you are traveling through Eastern Allegany County, not far from the Steuben County line.

All around you are the high, green hills. You come to a narrow valley, in which nestles a pretty village of many neat white houses and red tile roofs.

There seems to be a lot of bustle on the main street, considering it is a Sabbath afternoon and you are in a Western New York village. The Postoffice is open and so are most of the business places. There is even some washing flopping from a clothes line in a yard.

You are in a college town. For there are many young men and women carrying books and there are the Greek letters on the big old houses. There is a shady hillside campus, extending from the village street up into the woods. Modern brick and steel vie with white frame and native stone. A tall white tower, reminiscent of New England, glistens above the treetops.

Then across the valley floats the music of bells, the stately cadence of an old hymn. You are listening to the oldest carillon in the New World.

You are in Alfred, the York State village named for a Saxon king and one of the most interesting college towns in America.

Alfred has so many tile roofs because for years it was the home of terra cotta plants. The tile roofs are symbolic also of one of America's leading centers of education in the science of ceramics.

The Postoffice and the business places are open because so many of the villagers are Seventh Day Baptists who observe Saturday and not Sunday as a day of worship and rest. Otherwise the "Saturday keepers" of Alfred are no different than their neighbors who are "Sunday keepers." The Seventh Day Baptists are thrifty, tolerant people and had it not been for them, there would be no 120-acre campus, no 25 college buildings in Alfred Village.

There is more than one college but only one campus. The present setup is a bit bewildering to a stranger who had always thought of the village as the seat of 96-year-old Alfred University only.

Belonging wholly to the University, which has been from the beginning co-educational, nonsectarian and privately endowed, are the College of the Liberal Arts and the Graduate School, the latter organized in 1947. The University also conducts a summer session.

The New York State College of Ceramics, founded in 1900 as the State School of Clayworking and Ceramics, is a contract unit of the State University of New York and is state supported. However, it has always been administered under the law by the trustees of Alfred University and is considered an integral part of the University.

An entirely separate school is the New York State Agricultural and Technical Institute, established in 1908 as a State School of Agriculture and supported and administered by the state. It shares the campus and infirmary with the University. Ag-Tech students also use the Alfred assembly hall once a week. Otherwise the two institutions have no connections; with entirely distinct student bodies, faculties and courses.

The University has an enrollment of about 900, with more than 80 on its faculty. The Ag-Tech Institute has some 800 students and a teaching staff of 60. The population of Alfred is 2,053. The whole economy of the village revolves about its schools. Without them Alfred would revert to the hamlet it was before the first temple of learning opened in the settlement.

The first settlers were mostly Rhode Islanders and members of the Seventh Day Baptist denomination. They began arriving in the present township in 1807. Seventh Day Baptists also were pioneers in the towns of Almond and Andover.

There should be a memorial to Mrs. Henry Sheldon on the Alfred campus. It was she, who in 1836 when the pioneers decided to start a select school in Alfred, offered the north bedroom of her home for the project. Carpenters and mechanics of the village fitted the chamber into a class room and in the late Fall of 1836, the select school began its first 13-week term with 36 students. Out of that humble beginning grew Alfred University.

The students were charged a tuition fee of $3 and they had to bring their own books, slates and even chairs. A future president of Alfred, Jonathan Allen, then 13 years old, chopped six cords of wood to earn his tuition fee. The next year the settlers raised funds to erect a small, frame one-story school, which because of its strange-shaped cupola became known far and wide as "The Horned Bug."

An early principal was the Rev. James R. Irish, an evangelist of parts, who after he had added 200 members to the rolls of the Seventh Day Baptist Church, quit his pedagogical post to become its pastor. He was succeeded by a human dynamo of a man, William C. "Boss" Kenyon.

In 1843 the select school became an academy which made rapid strides under Kenyon. In 1857 the Seventh Day Baptists, comprising the bulk of the population of Alfred, joined with other residents in starting a collegiate and theological school. While it was launched under the banner of the Seventh Day church, it was to raise no barriers of creed or race. So Alfred University was chartered and "Boss" Kenyon became its first president. He died in 1867 while on a European trip and Jonathan Allen, the former student, who had become a teacher and a pillar of the school, took the helm.

For a quarter of a century, this almost legendary figure guided the young college in the back hills. Jonathan Allen was a physical and mental giant, a combined Paul Bunyon and Plato, a picturesque, patriarchal figure with a flowing beard, who left a lasting imprint on the college he loved.

With his own hands he helped grade the hillside campus, lay its walks and plant the pines he brought from the hills and the elms from the valleys. Within a radius of three miles of Alfred, he gathered some 7,000 stones, each one different, and made of them a miniature replica of a medieval German castle. It stands today at the edge of the woods, the Allen Steinheim Museum, one of the first college museums in the country. Allen gathered rare shells, Indian and pioneer relics and other curiosities that formed the nucleus of the present collection at Steinheim.

After Jonathan Allen died in 1892, the fortunes of Alfred went into a tailspin. Older supporters of the University were passing on. The treasury was low, enrollment was dropping, there was internal strife. The desperate trustees persuaded the urbane and astute pastor of the local church, the Rev. Boothe C. Davis, to assume the presidency.

For 38 years he served. The present Alfred is a monument to his energy and skill. First of all, he saw that to gain needed funds, friends and students, the University must widen its appeal and broaden its services.

One answer was the school of ceramics. Charles T. Harris, who operated one of the terra cotta plants in the village, is credited with first suggesting it. Doctor Davis was a persuasive man and in a state job in Albany there was John J. Merrill of Alfred, long a trustee of the University. So it came about that in 1900 the State Legislature passed a bill, carrying the necessary appropriation for a School of Clayworking and Ceramics at Alfred University. Charles F. Binns, an Englishman with life-long experience in the field, was made its first director. In 1932 the name of the school was changed to the State College of Ceramics.

Alfred today is best known nationally for its ceramics college, which has a wide recognition in industry. The ceramics department is housed in appropriately named Binns-Merrill Hall, which was dedicated at the 1952 commencement. It cost a million and a half dollars and is called the largest and most complete plant for ceramic education in the country.

Also in the realm of pure scholarship, the college which bears the name of the Saxon king who was "the good counselor," has an enviable standing. A recent nation-wide survey by the Ford Foundation to determine the number of scholars per 1,000 graduates, showed Alfred ranking sixth in the state.

Doctor Davis was succeeded in the presidency in 1933 by J. Nelson Norwood, who guided the college through 12 years of depression and war. The current "prexy" is M. Ellis Drake.

The University has a $660,000 expansion program under way with funds made available by bequests and by a Federal loan. It includes two new men's dormitories, additions to two others, two new wings for the Social Hall and a steel tower to replace the present derrick-like wooden framework that supports the famous Davis Memorial Carillon.

Those 35 Flemish bells were cast in the 16th and 17th centuries by noted founders. When during the first World War the Kaiser's armies were surging across the Lowlands, they were hidden in cellars, in attics and in the ground. The largest, weighing about 1,000 pounds, was buried for years under a tower in Luxembourg.

The late Dr. Lloyd Watson won renown in the scientific world for developing a method for the controlled mating of the honey bee. But on the Alfred campus and in the hearts of graduates and villagers, he always will be remembered as the man who brought the bells to Pine Hill.

Watson loved the music of bells and cherished the hope that somehow a carillon could be obtained for Alfred. He wrote an English bell founder, asking the price of a set. The price was pretty high. Each year thereafter the English company sent him a calendar with a picture of bells on it.

One day Mrs. Charlotte Greene of Boston came to the Watson home to buy some of the pure honey candy originated by Mrs. Watson. She noticed the calendar on the wall and said she was interested in carillons and knew where there were some ancient bells buried in Belgium. She promised that on her next trip abroad she would investigate the chances of obtaining some of them. She returned with the news that the bells were available. Some 400 Alfred alumni and friends raised the money and in July of 1937 the bells came to Pine Hill.

Through the gift of an Alfred trustee, John P. Herrick of Olean, eight more bells from the Lowlands soon will be added to the collection.

Only one man has ever played the Alfred bells. He is Dr.

Ray W. Wingate, a onetime president of the American Guild of Carillonneurs. Twice a week on Fridays and Sundays, he mounts the steps to the clavier 70 feet above the ground to send the sweet music floating across the valley.

The carillonneur is eagerly awaiting the new bells and their new steel pedestal. I am sure the high metal fence with the padlock on its gate will encircle the new installation as it does the present one. College boys will be college boys.

Oldest of the 25 buildings on the campus is big, stately, white Alumni Hall with its tall old fashioned tower. It was built in 1852 and for years was known as the Chapel. It now houses class rooms and an auditorium. Its floor boards creak noisily.

Another oldtimer hallowed by tradition is "The Brick," the girls' dorm. The old white building called The Gothic houses the School of Theology, about the only reminder, except the Saturday closing rule, of the Seventh Day Baptist origin of Alfred University.

Ever since 1933, St. Patrick's Day has brought a round of festivities to Alfred. "St. Pat's" is a traditional two-day festival, with parades of floats and costumed students, tea dances and open houses, climaxed by a grand ball. Then the engineering student chosen as "St. Pat," ascends the throne, along with the festival queen. The event is based on the tradition that St. Patrick is the patron saint of ceramic- and other-engineers, because, 'tis said, he used engineering devices to rid Erin of reptiles.

One day in 1909 Alfred President Davis held the handles of a horse-drawn plow breaking the ground for the new State School of Agriculture's only building. It now is the administration building of the Ag-Tech Institute and one of many on the campus. A two million dollar industrial building is under construction. Ag-Tech is on the march.

The school was authorized in 1908 to teach agriculture and home economics. The latter course was soon dropped. In recent years the emphasis has been on technical training.

A highlight of the school year is the Fall Festival. In November the institute holds open house and conducts tours for high school students, parents and representatives of industry and agriculture. In 1952 5,000 attended. Some of them came 200 to 300 miles, by the busload.

Director of Ag-Tech is the widely known Paul B. Orvis, a one-time student at the school and at the close of World War II director of food distribution for 17 European countries under the Marshall Plan. He also was the man who fed the American sector of Berlin after V-E day.

A friendly, informal air pervades the whole Alfred campus. It is no place for snobs or playboys. The breezes that come down from the high green hills are fresh and clean and typify the spirit of Alfred.

The Alfred University Bank is said to be the only bank in the country which is open Sundays. For the first time in its 70 years, the bank was closed Sundays during July and August in 1953. The old schedule was resumed the first Sunday in September.

The Postoffice at Alfred is open all day Sunday and open Saturdays only for a half hour in the late afternoon for the sale of stamps and mailing parcel post. The Postoffice at Alfred Station, another Seventh Day Baptist stronghold, has the same unusual schedule. It took an act of Congress many years ago to put it into effect.

Alfred is 1,800 feet above sea level and that makes it one of the highest incorporated villages in the state. One hill in the township has an elevation of 2,350 feet. South of Alfred is the highest point on the Erie Railroad, 1,776 feet above tidewater. The name of that point is Tip Top.

Farther south is the tidy village of Andover, another Allegany County community where the Seventh Day Baptists settled. Andover has one of the handsomest high schools in the Tier. It is stately, of red brick with white trim and with a tower. Travelers on Route 17 will remember the two-mile long hill between Greenwood, in Steuben County and Andover and the oil pumps along the road in that wild and wooded countryside.

Almond, Alfred's northern neighbor hugging the Steuben County line, for more than a quarter of a century was the scene of "The World's Horse Traders' Convention," a unique institution. George Kase of Almond, who has been trading horses ever since he was knee high to a colt, started it with only five horses.

He built up his David Harumish extravaganza to the point where in 1953 the convention was moved from its traditional Almond setting to the County Fairgrounds at Angelica, with a lot of sidelights, such as a hill-billy revue and a horse-pulling contest. The Kase farm, outside of Almond on the road to Angelica, just isn't big enough any more.

Dealers come from all over the East and Midwest, some from the Kentucky "Blue Grass." But they bring mostly saddle horses now in their big vans. Time was, before the world became motorized, that draft horses were in the majority. One convention, held on the McHenry Valley Road, drew 5,000 people.

This is like no other convention anywhere. There are no committee sessions, no long winded oratory, just the chant of the auctioneer and the sharp battle of wits that goes with horse-trading—and with draw poker.

Chapter 19

Wellsville and the Oil Country

One June day in 1879 the editor of Beers' History of Allegany County dropped his pencil and leaned back in his chair. He had just sent the last pages of that voluminous work to the printer. Now he could relax.

Just then an assistant dashed in with a newspaper clipping. It contained news so momentuous that the editor called the copy back and hastily wrote this appendix to the county history, under the heading

STRIKING OIL

"The following from the *Elmira Gazette* of June 21, 1879, received as the last pages of this work are about to go to press, is our only information of the decided success of O. P. Taylor's enterprise in boring for petroleum:

" 'There is no disguising the fact that oil has been found at Wellsville and in paying quantities. Triangle Well . . . four and one half miles southwest from Wellsville . . . was commenced April 17. . . . At 1,109 feet the oil-bearing sand was reached. . . . The drill stopped at 1,117. June 12 the well was torpedoed with a 20-quart shot of glycerine when the oil was sent 20 to 30 feet over the derrick. Saturday came the flow since which time there has flowed between 8 and 10 barrels a day. The well is certainly a gusher. Sunday brought a crowd. The place was named Triangle City. Four lager beer stands were started. The town is filling up with strangers. Letters, telegrams and inquiries are pouring in. Look out for a great big city at Wellsville.' "

The editor showed sound judgment in making that breathless, last-minute addition to the History of Allegany County. That "gusher" at Triangle City in June of 1879 was one of the most significant events in Allegany County's history.

It ushered in a new and golden age, especially for Wellsville and the southern tier of towns. It also brought the wildest, hell-roaring period in the history of Allegany.

After Colonel Drake's epochal oil strike at Titusville in 1859, oil men bored into many corners of Allegany's rugged terrain for the "liquid gold." They brought in only dry wells or unprofitable ones.

But Taylor's Triangle No. 1 in the Town of Scio made history. It was the first productive commerical well in Allegany County. It started a mad boom. Triangle City sprang up where had been a barren field. Derricks began to dot the countryside.

Orville P. Taylor, the man who started it all, had been making and selling cigars in Wellsville before he went into the oil business. He had put down two wells that were failures before he hit the jackpot with Triangle No. 1. He had put all that he had, all he could borrow into its drilling. His wife had sold her jewelry to raise the money to complete the venture. During the second World War the memory of this oil pioneer who would not give up, who has been called "The Colonel Drake of the Allegany field," was honored by the government when it named a Liberty ship the Orville P. Taylor.

The oil madness reached its apogee in Richburg in 1881. That village, named after a settler and without any prophetic allusion, had slept the years away on the shady road that led over the hills between Bolivar and Friendship. It had some 25 buildings and less than 200 inhabitants. The arrival of the horse-drawn stage with the mail and an occasional passenger was the big event of the day.

On April 27, 1881, a gusher came in one mile west of the village and Richburg no longer was a crossroads hamlet. For a little over a year it was the wildest, wickedest boom town in America. Oil scouts spread the news of the strike and the invasion was on. Oil men came pouring across the border from Pennsylvania, from all points of the compass, along with the unsavory army of camp followers of both sexes that in those days accompanied the discovery of new oil fields. There was a wild scramble for leases. In a week Richburg's population soared from 200 to 8,000.

In less than a week after the oil discovery, four stage lines were operating into Pennsylvania. Big old fashioned stages, drawn by four horses, came lumbering into Richburg, laden with oil-crazed passengers. Flimsy houses, stores with false fronts, saloons and gambling dens sprang up.

Men slept in hay mows, under the maples of the little park near the village schoolhouse, on billiard tables. The village grist mill became a bagnio and at one time there were 135 women plying the oldest profession in the world. There were gambling hells in barns, over stores. Money flowed like water. There were murders and stabbings and gang fights. No mining camp in the West was wilder.

Narrow gauge railroads were hastily built over the hills. An opera house mushroomed on Main Street. Fay Templeton appeared there and so did John L. Sullivan. Picturesque adventurers came to town, like Samuel Boyle, whose favorite stunt was to ride his horse under a flaming open gas flare, reach up, light his cigar with a dollar bill and canter away.

Farmers on whose lands oil had been struck became rich overnight. Men who had not seen more than $50 at one time in their lives counted their wealth in the thousands. One man who did not trust banks took out his lease money in gold, shoved it into grain sacks and sat up all night beside it, with a rifle. Another, who all his life had yearned to own a fine gold watch, bought four of them, one for each vest pocket.

Richburg's day of glory was short-lived. In the Summer of 1882 came word of a rich new strike at Cherry Grove, Warren County, Pennsylvania. At once the fickle army that followed the oil fields, deserted Richburg. The boom town sank back into slumber. The opera house was converted into a cheese factory and later burned. Some of the buildings fell into decay. Some were moved away.

The secondary recovery of the oil fields through "flooding" revived the industry in the hills around Richburg. Until recently there was an oil pump chugging away in a church yard there. Today Richburg is just a drowsy village, dreaming of the Babylon of the oil country that it was in 1881.

Down the valley to the southward, Richburg's neighbor, Bolivar, named after the South American liberator when it was incorporated a village in 1825, shared the bonanza of the 1880s. In ten months in the hectic year of '81, its population rocketed from 160 to 4,500. But it weathered the exodus to Cherry Grove that all but killed Richburg.

Bolivar's economy was built more solidly and the rejuvenation of the oil industry through "flooding" gave Bolivar a new and lasting prosperity. This village of 1,500 is one of the wealthiest communities per capita in the state.

There were nine graduates in the class of 1893 of the Bolivar Academy. The honor student was a 17-year-old lad named Frank Gannett. His father ran a hotel in the oil town and young Frank found time from his studies and his odd jobs, which included delivering out-of-town newspapers and sending an occasional local story to the Buffalo dailies, to play in the village cornet band and to catch on the village baseball nine. Other players on that team were Fielder Jones and Pat Dougherty. Both became big leaguers. So did Frank Gannett but in the field of publishing and public affairs, not on the baseball diamond.

Out of the madness of the boom days, Wellsville emerged as the capital of the Allegany oil fields, one of the most prosperous, substantial, brisk and attractive communities in Upstate New York with a population of nearly 6,500. Wellsville shrugs off depressions. As long as the oil pumps chug away in the hills around it and the pipe lines bring in the crude to the huge Sinclair refinery in the oil capital, Wellsville's economy is as solid as old South Hill, the 2,300 foot high gatekeeper at the end of its principal street.

Southern Allegany County also is one of the state's most reliable sources of natural gas. In early days gas had no great recovery value and farmers used the surplus from the wells for huge outdoor lights that burned all night in the barnyards. The gas fields are chiefly on the fringe of the oil pools.

Hazards ever lurk in a land of derricks and pumps, of tanks and pipe lines full of highly inflammable liquid. Wellsville won't soon forget the refinery fire of June 17, 1938, which brought death to three spectators and injuries to 42 others. A naphtha tank exploded and sailed 200 feet across the Genesee, scattering blazing oil and flying steel on the crowd gathered on the river bank. That million dollar fire raged for most of two days.

Then in 1940 there was the gas well that ran wild south of Wellsville. It was a tremendous spectacle. At first the runaway gas shot straight in the air. Later it fanned out. The loss was enormous and the fire hazard was great. To stem the flow and avert a fire, a crew of specialists was imported from Texas. They used weighted mud, heavier than the gas pressure, to tame the mad "gusher."

The oil well "shooter" flirts with sudden death most of his working hours. For he is handling nitroglycerin. In the old days he used to haul his lethal cargo to the derricks in a horse-drawn wagon over rough roads. Some villages banned the "torpedo wagons" from their streets. Nowadays motor trucks do the job. More than one "shooter" has been blown to bits, sometimes on the way to the derrick, sometimes while "shooting" the well.

Nitroglycerin first came into general use in 1867 as the explosive charge in the torpedo which dislodges the well-clogging paraffin and enlarges the cavity in the oil sands.

The "shooter" lowers the tin shells, filled with nitro, into the hole, after fitting a firing head to the top shell. Then he drops a "go devil," a heavy iron weight, into the well and runs. The "go-devil" clatters down the casing, strikes the firing head and explodes the shot. Then comes a dull boom, from way "down under." A plume of oil and gas rises, feebly at first, then with accumulated force, it shoots high above the derrick and splashes over the surrounding terrain. If the well is dry or a dud, nothing happens or at best, only a puny column spurts out. In those cases, somebody has lost a lot of money.

All is not glamor or royalties in the oil fields. I think this bit of verse from the pen of Mrs. Louise Stuck, of Richburg, whose husband works in the oil fields and who lives in the heart of the Allegany belt, tells the story well:

> *"Whenever a derrick towers into the blue,*
> *Whenever the sand gives forth its precious spoil*
> *Of inky, sluggish, hidden streams of oil—*
> *Here is toil and sweat and heartache, too."*

Methodism and Mammon mingle on a church lawn in the village of Allentown, southwest of Wellsville, in the hills where the pumps and lines are thick. There, beside the old white Methodist Church with the square tower, is a large wayside sign bearing the name of the church and this message: "God First Always." Just behind the sign is an oil pump.

* * *

The first settler in the township of Wellsville—and in Allegany County—was Nathaniel Dike of Connecticut, who had graduated from Yale and had served on Washington's staff. In 1795 he built a cabin along the stream which ever since has been known as Dike's Creek.

The site of Wellsville village on the Genesee River was not settled until 1831. Then a score of pioneers met to select a name for the settlement. They decided on Wellsville, in honor of Gardner Wells, who, 'tis said, was the only resident not at the meeting. About 80 years ago there was an attempt to rename the village Genesee.

The pine on the hills provided an early source of revenue. Then tanneries and cheese factories were built. And in 1851 the Erie Railroad came to give the village its biggest boom—until Triangle Well No. 1 came roaring in, back in 1879, to start Wellsville on the road to affluence.

Besides the big Sinclair refinery, this bustling little city numbers among its industries, the large plants of the Air Preheater Corporation and of the Worthington Pump and Machinery Company. Recently the Bausch & Lomb Optical Company of Rochester opened a branch plant in Wellsville.

The tourists on Routes 17 and 19 which intersect at Wellsville don't see "The Pink House" at West State and South Brooklyn Streets, on the west side of town. I have never seen that exact shade of paint on any other building anywhere.

It is mauve or lavender and not pink, despite the name Wellsville people have given it. The ornate brick residence with the scroll work and fancy trimmings is trimmed in white.

It has worn that spectacular coat ever since it was built some 80 years ago by the late druggist, E. B. Hall, who also had a paint business. The particular pigment needed for its paint formula can be obtained only in Italy. "The Pink House" got no new coat during World War II. The Hall will stipulated that no other color ever be used. The driveway entrance is guarded by two angelic figures and the doorway by twin lions. Hall's daughter, Mrs. J. M. Carpenter, resides in "The Pink House" and every Christmas time she follows an old tradition. The house and grounds are ablaze with many-colored lights.

Wellsville is proud of its fine public library, a memorial to David A. Howe, an oil man, and of its new and modern, 75-bed, $1,300,000 hospital. It would be proud of its entry in the PONY League if the team would climb out of the second division.

It has reason to be proud of some of the men and women who were born in that neighborhood, people like Charles M. Sheldon, author of a religious book, "In His Steps," which was one of the best sellers of all time; Grace Livingston Hill, writer of popular fiction; Adam McMullen, onetime Governor of Nebraska; Raymond N. Ball, president of Rochester's largest bank, and last, but by no means least, George "Gabby" Hayes, the darling of the television tots, who was born in 1883 on a hilltop farm in the nearby Town of Alma.

* * *

The magic Seneca Oil Spring was known the length and breadth of the old Indian domain long before any white man ever saw it and before it went into the white man's records as the place where petroleum first was discovered in America.

The historic spring is on the mile-square Oil Spring Indian Reservation which straddles the Cattaraugus-Allegany line and is near the village of Cuba in the latter county.

About it clings an ancient Seneca legend. It was the original pool of oil or fat into which all animals were driven to make them fat. The Good Spirit caught such as he thought should not be fat and stripped them of their oil. Among those doomed to be forever lean were the wolf, the mink, the otter and the skunk. Favored beasts were the bear, buffalo and beaver.

There is another, more earthy Indian legend about the origin of petroleum. One day a very fat squaw waddled to the Oil Spring for water. The ground was soft and she slipped into the spring. She never was seen again. Ever since oil has risen to the surface of the Oil Spring.

In 1627 a Franciscan missionary, Father Joseph de la Roche d'Allion wrote of a visit he made to the Indians in what is now Western New York. His narrative contained these words: "They have squashes . . . and very good oil."

There is no positive record the friar ever visited the Seneca Oil Spring but the medicinal properties of its oil were widely known among the Indians and d'Allion likely saw the tribesmen using oil which came from the magic spring. At any rate the date 1627 has been accepted as the first printed record of petroleum in America and the Seneca Oil Spring as the birthplace of the industry.

In 1721 Joncaire the elder, France's "ambassador" to the Senecas, visited the Oil Spring. In 1767 oil from the pool was sent to Sir William Johnson for treatment of a wound the lord of the Mohawk Valley had suffered at Niagara. Several

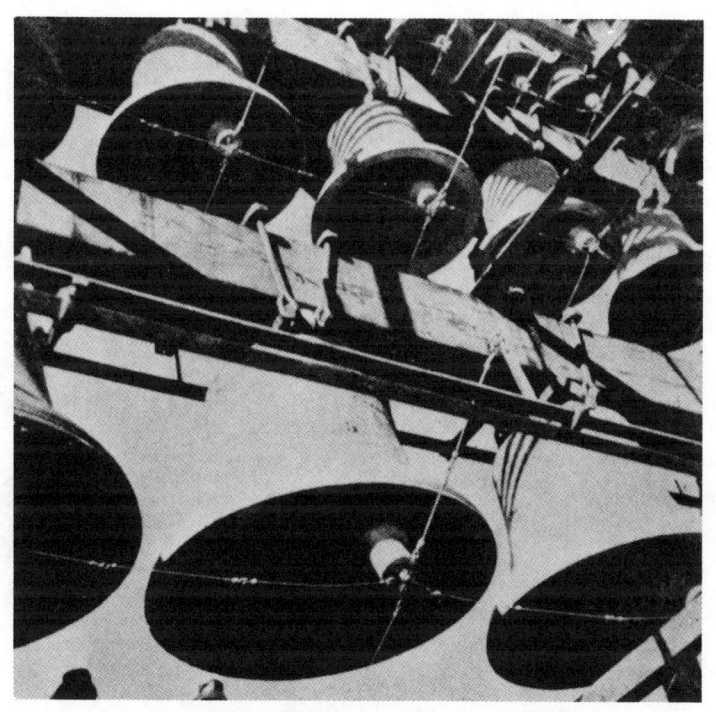

Alfred's Carillon, Oldest in America

Grape Harvest Along Keuka Lake

Indian trails led to the spring in the forest with the scum floating on its surface.

In pioneer times the Indians gathered the oil by spreading blankets over the spring and wringing out of the blankets the oil they had soaked up. They caught the oil in vessels, transferred it to small vials and then bartered it with the white settlers, who sold it in drug stores as "Seneca Oil, good for man or beast."

After the Titusville strike of 1859, the oil hunters turned to the region of the famous spring on which oil had floated for centuries. In December, 1859, a lease was negotiated with the Seneca Nation which owned the Oil Spring, as it does today.

Sometime late in 1860 or early in 1861, three borings were made near the Oil Spring. Two were "dusters." The third well yielded a small quantity of oil, which was bottled and sold as a medicine, a lubricant and a vermin killer for livestock. Oil has never been struck in paying quantities around the traditional place of its discovery in America.

On July 23, 1927, in observance of the tercentenary of the friar's account of the first petroleum in the New World, a marker was dedicated at the Oil Spring by national and state petroleum associations, with members of the Franciscan order and the Seneca Nation taking part.

The historic spring itself, at the edge of a dark and swampy wood, is a fenced-in, stagnant pool, 18 feet in diameter, ringed by an iron-bound cask which has been preserved by the oil in the water. The wooden staves of the barrel are slowly rotting away.

No Seneca has lived on the Oil Spring Reservation since 1937. In 1920 four were in shacks there. In early times the Indians regarded the site more highly. The chiefs howled when, through an oversight, it was not included among the reservations set aside in the Treaty of Big Tree in 1797. Before the council disbanded, Thomas Morris, son of Robert, signed a paper granting the Senecas the mile-square tract forever.

Three years later Joseph Ellicott, the Holland Land Company agent, gave the Senecas a map on which the reservations, including the Oil Spring, were marked in red. For years it was thought the old map had been lost. When in 1855 a white settler sought title to land he had cleared there, the map came out of old Chief Blacksnake's deer-hide trunk to win the case in the Court of Appeals for the Seneca Nation.

A little north of the Oil Spring, 1,665 feet above sea level and sparkling among the hulking hills is a 500-acre lake. It is man-made but none the less beautiful. It was called the largest artificial lake in the world in 1858 when the State of New York constructed it at a cost of $150,000 as a feeder for the Genesee Valley and Erie Canals. The huge earth dam built then is now overgrown with shrubs and trees.

After the Genesee Valley Canal was abandoned in 1878, the state continued to maintain the lake, which now is under the supervision of the Allegany State Park Commission. On its shores are some 400 cottages. The lake is a favorite vacation resort for Olean people. Generations have danced at the pavilion operated by generations of the Olive family.

Cuba village, two miles south of the lake, is in the township of the same name which originally was Oil Creek, after the stream which flows through it.

The last spike in the Erie Railroad was driven at Cuba, where the tracks from Dunkirk on the west and at Piermont on the east were joined in 1851. When the first train arrived in Cuba in May of that year with President Fillmore, Daniel

Webster et al aboard, the man who had driven that spike, Daniel Kirkpatrick, superintendent of the road, ordered his men to blockade the track with ties until Webster changed his mind about making a speech at Cuba. "The Godlike Daniel" changed his mind and spoke.

Cuba has always been a center of the dairying industry and half a century and more ago the Cuba cheese market set the price for a considerable area.

* * *

Friendship—what more pleasing name could be bestowed upon a village and a town? Friendship's neighboring town to the east is Amity. If Freedom, Bliss and Protection could only be moved down there. But Friendship Village was such a rough place in its early youth that it was called Bloody Corners.

Friendship village is not in, but of the Oil Country. No pumps bang away on its lawns or churchyards. But it has played its part in the story of oil in Allegany County. Friendship men, among them the Miners and the Wellmans, helped develop the oil fields of the Southern Tier.

And in Friendship the first oil refinery in the county was built in 1881, the year of the Richburg boom. Two years later, John, son of Sidney Rigdon, the noted Mormon, bought into the company. The plant prospered but some neighbors complained of its offensive odors. There were veiled threats. One night Mrs. Rigdon and her daughter, Jessie Secord, from their home near the refinery, watched the plant go up in smoke with all its stored oil and refined products. It never was rebuilt. A strange happening in a village with the name of Friendship.

Other strange things have happened in Friendship village. At its Main and East Water Streets, stands a tall white house with gables and porches. There are iron bars across some of its windows.

The man who put them there was George W. Robinson. He has been dead these 75 years and his secret died with him. He was one of three Mormon exiles who came to Friendship around 1847, after their leader, Joseph Smith, was slain by a mob in Illinois. The others were Edward B. Wingate and Sidney Rigdon. Ned Wingate, who, like Robinson, had married a Rigdon daughter, had been an officer of the Danites, the Mormon secret police.

Sidney Rigdon had climbed high in the hierarchy of the church. He once was second in command to Joseph the Prophet. Some have maintained that he, and not Smith, wrote the *Book of Mormon*. To the day of his death in Friendship village in 1876, Rigdon stoutly denied that story.

When he came to Friendship, where another daughter lived, he was a broken, beaten man, cast out by the church he had helped to found. He had lost a dramatic battle for the mantle of the slain Joseph to Brigham Young.

In the Allegany County village, Robinson, who reputedly had been a fiscal officer in the Mormon church, became an important citizen. He built a brick store and a mill and became a bank president. The villagers called him "General" and his handsome house was the showplace of the town.

But no one ever found out what fear drove the prosperous "General" to bar the ground-floor rear windows of that house or what treasure he guarded there, not even trusting the vaults of his own bank.

Village gossip, snowballing through the years, has built up tales of secret documents and money bags behind the barred windows. One story concerns the appearance of two strange men in Friendship village. They were looking for the onetime fiscal officer of the Church of Jesus Christ of

Latter Day Saints. Hearing of their arrival, Robinson, so the story goes dashed to his home, grabbed up a satchel and boarded a train for Buffalo. On his return the strangers had left. It was then the iron bars were placed on the windows of the tall white house.

Another tradition has Robinson barring his windows, because of his fear, an echo of old feuds within the church, that some vengeful visitor might come to do him bodily harm, perhaps even take his life.

Probably no one will ever know why "The General" barred his windows. But after these years the bars are still there.

Chapter 20

Old "Stew-ben"

Steuben is the only one of the four western counties of the Southern Tier whose name is not of Indian derivation. It was named after the Prussian officer who trained Washington's raw troops, after "the Drillmaster of the Revolution," Baron Freidrich Wilhelm Ludolf Gerhard Augustin von Steuben. The baron never pronounced his family name "Stew-ben."

But the York State pioneers did not care a whoop about fancy European titles or pronunciations and so to this day the Southern Tier county of loidly hills and wide valleys has been called "Stew-ben."

It is the oldest of the four western counties. A child of old mother Ontario, its birth certificate is dated 1796. Its godfather was Charles Williamson, courtly land agent for British interests with more than a million acres to sell and to settle.

The first name picked for the new county was not Steuben, but Schuyler, in honor of another Revolutionary general, Philip Schuyler. But Schuyler, then a member of the State Legislature, declined the honor. Many years later when the general was no longer around to object, another county, some of it sliced off Steuben, was named in his honor.

Steuben is the largest in area (1,408 square miles) of all the counties of the Southern Tier. It is so big that it is one of the few counties in the nation to have three courthouses.

The stately village of Bath has been the shire town from the beginning, but since 1853 court terms have been held in Corning, "The Crystal City," world center of the technical and art glass industry, and since 1902, in Hornell, "The Maple City," and longtime railroad center.

Before the white man came, an oaken post, carved and strangely painted, was a landmark of the Indian empire. It stood where three rivers met and where the Indian trail forked, the present site of the industrial village of Painted Post. It was near the Painted Post that the first white man's cabin in the county arose in 1784. For a time the whole region was called "The District of the Painted Post."

As in its sister counties, lumbering was a major industry in the early time. But agriculture ever has been the real bulwark of Steuben's economy. The county ranks second in the state in the production of potatoes and second only to Chautauqua in grape production.

Steuben is the only Southern Tier county that contains any part of a Finger Lake. Both of Keuka's lovely arms dip into its borders. Along the two-pronged lake with its romantic memories of steamboat days, flourishes a vast wine industry, with Hammondsport, which also was a cradle of aviation, as its capital. The vineyards on the hills and the old stone wineries give this corner of New York State a distinctive Old World charm.

The census of 1950 showed 91,439 people living in Steuben County. I could not meet all of them, but I did talk with scores of them. And I did not find a single one who was other than gracious and friendly—and loyally proud of the grand old county of "Stew-ben."

Chapter 21

Where Potato Is King

Gravy, not glamor, is generally associated with the potato. One of the most common and humble of vegetables, the "spud" is hardly an exotic.

Yet I think there are elements of drama in the remarkable renaissance of the potato industry in Northern Steuben County in the last 15 years. There King Spud is back on his throne. Back of his comeback is the story of an "invasion," some modern pioneers and the conquest of stony hills, some of them 2,000 feet above the level of the sea.

Ever since the days of the Indians, potatoes have been grown in Steuben County. The county was one of the first large commercial tuber-growing areas in the nation. As early as 1852, the first carload was shipped out of Wayland.

The Boggs potato grader was invented in Steuben and is still being made in the village of Atlanta. The Rosch digger, standard equipment on farms at the turn of the century, was developed in Steuben County, as was the Spalding Rose, an early and popular variety of potato.

As late as 1910, some 30,000 acres of the county's rugged terrain were planted to potatoes. But by 1930 the acreage had dwindled to 17,000, with an average yield of 125 bushels to the acre. The overworked soil had grown tired. So apparently had some of the potato farmers. Today the acreage is no more than in 1930 but the yield is 400 bushels to the acre, thanks to the "invasion."

In 1937 William Stempfle, then Steuben County agricultural agent, concerned over the waning production, called a meeting at Bath in an effort to revitalize one of the county's leading crops. His missionary work resulted in inquiries from two young Maine men, partners in the growing and shipping of potatoes at Caribou, in the heart of the rich Aroostook potato belt. Romeyn Babbin, then 25, and Jack Bishop, then 27, were impressed by Stempfle's recital of Steuben's past yields and the possibilties for future ones.

They decided to gamble on the Steuben soil and in 1938 rented 23 acres in the Wayland area, which they planted to potatoes. Their methods were considered revolutionary in Western New York and local skeptics were numerous.

The skeptics were confounded, for the yield was good. The newcomers' success lay in their methods—large plantings, deep plowing, use of superior seed, liberal use of fertilizer, extensive spraying and dusting, rotation of crops and highly mechanized operations.

Other families from Maine joined the potato growing colony which became known as "Little Maine." Then came growers from Long Island where expanding urbanization is crowding out the potato fields. The Long Islanders also went in for cabbages, cauliflower, cucumbers and rutabagas. Muck potato farming is a success in the Prattsburg area.

The principal towns of Steuben's resurgent "potato kingdom" are Wayland, Cohocton, Avoca, Fremont, Howard, Hornell and Dansville. Many local farmers have joined "the spud parade" and are adopting the methods used so successfully by the "invaders."

Today the annual yield in the county is in excess of five million bushels. Steuben, second only to Nassau among the potato-growing counties of the state, raises a third of the Upstate crop.

The potato renaissance has enhanced the general prosperity of the region. Long vacant warehouses and factories have been converted into potato storages. The countryside is dotted with these enormous structures, housing millions of bushels. At harvest time the convoys of trucks, bringing the potatoes to the warehouses, choke the highways. The harvest brings into the region an army of migrant workers, mostly Southern Negroes and West Indians. They are housed in camps on the potato farms. Many of them stay into the Winter, sorting, grading and loading at the warehouses.

The banners of the "Potato Kingdom," the white blossoms, wave triumphantly these Summers on rocky plateaus 2,000 feet above tidewater.

* * *

In the far northwestern corner of Steuben County, nature stages a grand show the year around.

There 554 acres of unspoiled natural beauty have been preserved as Stony Brook State Park. It is on State Highway 36, the Dansville-Hornell highway and is three miles south of the village of Dansville. It is barely within Steuben's borders, only one mile south of the Livingston County line. The park was acquired by the state in 1928. At that time it embraced only 251 acres.

Stony Brook dashes down from the high hills, over three waterfalls, between rocky cliffs, in places 200 feet above the cold, pure water, and through a wooded glen. The park has two fresh-water swimming pools and a camping site. It is a favorite picnic spot for people of the region. If you like to climb and your wind is good, there is a picturesque mile-long trail along the canyon's rim.

Once a great railroad bridge, touted as the highest in the world, straddled the gorge. It was built in 1907 by the Pittsburgh, Shawmut & Northern Railroad. Soon after the bridge was built, an awed crowd in the glen watched Warren "Speck" Allen of the famous daredevil tribe of Dansville "Flying Allens" parachute safely from its 330-feet height, wearing a derby hat. In 1948 the last Shawmut train rumbled over the high bridge. Now there are only the crumbling abutments.

* * *

In the year of 1848, a new township was formed from the western part of Cohocton. It had to have a name and Supervisor John Hess was given the task of choosing one. First he proposed Millville but the State Legislature rejected it, because there already was a Millville in the state. So Hess had to try again. He had a deadline to meet. The legislative session was drawing to a close.

He and his friend, Myron Patchin, the peace justice, went into executive session. For hours they mulled over names. Patchin chanced to whistle a few bars of the hymn, "Wayland." Suddenly he cried out: "John, I've got it. The name is Wayland."

Wayland has been the name ever since, not only of the township, but also of its principal village. Wayland is the biggest village in the potato belt with a population of 1,834.

Many of its early settlers were thrifty Germans. They gave a solid character to the place which it still retains. Wayland is a comfortable, homey village, sailing on a pretty even keel.

Wayland has shared in the prosperity of the resurgent potato belt and is an important shipping and storage point in King Spud's domain. For half a century the kingpin of its economy has been the W. H. Gunlocke Company. Gunlocke chairs are sold all over the world. The plant started with six employees. Now it has nearly 400.

August 30, 1943 is a date the village will never forget. The name of Wayland was splashed in headlines all over the land—because of a great disaster. One mile west of the village, the crack Lackawanna Flyer, roaring westward at high speed, struck a switch engine, inexplicably on the main track. Many victims were trapped in the wrecked coaches and scalded by live steam from the locomotive boiler. The toll eventually reached 29 dead and 150 injured.

Near Perkinsville in the early 1900s one of the largest mastadons ever found in the state was unearthed. It now is on display at the State Museum at Albany.

Once bustling Patchin Mills is only a roadside sign and a huddle of buildings now. Grass covers the tracks where the late Bert Patchin trained his show horses and his trotters. His widow, the vivacious Sally, lives on the ancestral acres. Through the years her hand-painted baskets and pottery have brought many feet to her studio door. Some of her visitors have been famous ones—among them Lily Pons, Roger Babson, George Eastman, Bernarr Macfadden.

In the southern part of Wayland township, on the road to Hornell, Loon Lake sparkles, a gem among the hills. Its shores are lined with summer cottages, mostly those of Hornell folk. It long has been a playspot of the region.

Conhocton, an Indian word meaning "log in the water," is the name of a Steuben county river. But when the pioneers came to name a town through which it courses, they dropped the "n" and we have the town of Cohocton and the villages of Cohocton and North Cohocton. North Cohocton and Atlanta are as close together as two potatoes in a hill. Atlanta, called Blood's Station in the old days after a pioneer, is on the railroad. North Cohocton isn't.

Tourists on Route 15 will remember Cohocton as the village with the mile-long Main Street. Albertus Larrowe built in his home town the largest buckwheat flouring mill in the world. The Larrowe Corporation still has a big buckwheat mill in the village.

From a Cohocton farm came Orson Squire Fowler, high priest of phrenology a century ago when the "science" of reading human character in the bumps of human heads, was in flower. He went to New York and wrote books and lectured on the subject. He took his sister, Charlotte, and his brother, Lorenzo, with him and they shared in his gold and glory.

Land Agent Williamson's road builders blazed a tree at every mile in the Conhocton Valley. North Cohocton was at the '22-mile tree," denoting its distance from Bath. Cohocton was at the "18-mile tree" and Avoca was at the "eight-mile" marker. Avoca did not always have its romantic name. Once it was Podunk. Legend says the name was changed at the behest of a woman on her death bed.

Another yarn is told about Eight Mile Creek near Avoca. A pioneer who lived along that stream wanted to drive the Indians from his hunting ground. So he cut several limbs and branches from trees, bored auger holes in them, filled the apertures with gunpowder, carefully plugged the holes, strewed the "loaded" firewood in the forest—and waited. As he expected, the Indians picked up the firewood left in their path. But when they ignited it, the fire exploded in their faces. Believing the woods bewitched, they left that particular hunting ground to the white man.

* * *

The potato belt villages of Prattsburg and Wheeler are linked with one of America's most stirring sagas, the trek of missionaries Marcus Whitman and his bride, Narcissa, to the Oregon country in the first wagon to cross the Rockies, the part they played in the winning of the West and their death as martyrs in Indian massacre.

Narcissa Prentiss was born in Prattsburg in 1808, the daughter of a business man-judge. She grew up into a queenly, golden-haired girl with a strong, clear soprano voice. She sang in the village choir. She was a devout girl and yearned to become a missionary.

A fellow student at Prattsburg's Franklin Academy, which has kept its old name all these years, was Henry Spalding, a lanky youth who lived at nearby Wheeler. His ambition was to be a preacher and the story is he was a rejected suitor for Narcissa's hand. Perhaps the old judge frowned upon him because he was born out of wedlock.

Be that as it may, Narcissa married Marcus Whitman, a determined and vigorous young doctor, a native of Rushville, who practiced medicine for a time at Wheeler. He shared Narcissa's desire for missionary work and after he had been appointed a medical missionary for the Presbyterian Church to the Cayuse Indians in far Oregon, he and Narcissa were married. Immediately after the ceremony in 1835, the young couple left on their perilous journey.

Oddly enough, Spalding, the jilted suitor, went along. He was then a minister and married. His wife accompanied him. It was Spalding's light wagon that made the historic trip over the Rockies.

The trek to Oregon is a familiar story. Over a trail known only to Indians and fur traders, across the blazing plains and through the lonely mountain passes, the little band went—by wagon most of the way. Narcissa Whitman and Eliza Spalding were the first white women ever to travel the Oregon Trail. After them was to come a mighty stream of covered wagons.

For eleven troubled years the Whitmans maintained their

mission near the present Walla Walla, Wash., in territory then claimed both by the United States and England.

In 1847 an epidemic struck the Cayuses. Despite Doctor Whitman's best efforts, many of them died. The superstitious Indians blamed the white doctor for the plague. He was a doomed man and he knew it. But he stuck to his post. Then one gray November afternoon the savages struck at the mission house. They killed Whitman and Narcissa and 12 others. The story of their martyrdom stirred the nation and had much to do with making Oregon a territory of the United States.

Now there are monuments in many states to Marcus Whitman and places and colleges bear his name.

In the Upstate hills where they were born, the martyrs are not forgotten. Out of Rushville winds a Marcus Whitman Highway and out of Prattsburg a Narcissa Prentiss Highway. The white house in Prattsburg where Narcissa was born 145 years ago belongs to the Missionary Board of the Presbyterian Church and is used as a home for retired missionaries. The widow of one lives there now.

And in little Wheeler, there's a marker at the place where young Doctor Whitman had his office and another along the road to Bath where Henry Spaulding was born. It tells how he died, at the age of 72, as he had lived, ministering to the Indians in the Far West.

Prattsburg has kept alive the memory of the frontier heroine, the blond girl who sang in the village choir. Narcissa Prentiss Hall is the name of the basement community meeting place in the Presbyterian Church.

According to tradition, at the Whitmans' marriage, all the guests rose to sing in farewell Narcissa's favorite hymn, "My Native Land I Love Thee." Thinking of the perilous journey ahead of the young couple, the singers were overcome by emotion and the voices quavered—all but one. The clear, strong soprano of Narcissa carried on the song to the end.

And now at church and community gatherings in the village of her nativity, they still sing Narcissa's song.

Prattsburg, comely village with a shady public square, is the terminus of one of the few remaining short-line railroads, the 11.4 mile single track line which connects with the Erie at Kanona. It began in 1889 as the Kanona and Prattsburg. A locomotive called "Old Huldy" hauled the first train. Fifty years to the day after its maiden trip, "Old Huldy" gave way to a new locomotive. The bell of the original engine is preserved in the Prattsburg depot.

Until 1929 three passenger trains were running daily each way. Then the Prattsburg Railroad Corporation, formed in 1917 by local interests, organized a bus line which it still owns and operates between Prattsburg and Bath.

Now there is no fixed schedule on the little railroad. Whenever there is freight to haul, a gas-powered engine hauls it. Potatoes and onions, grown in the region, form the principal cargo. The busiest season is from September to April. The little road has a powerful competitor in the motor truck.

A refreshing old fashioned American spirit of rugged individualism still lives in this 11-mile Steuben County railroad—in an age of speed, monopoly and absentee ownership.

One of the stations along the railroad is called Beans. It does not get its name from the field vegetable. The Bean family of Geneva bought a farm along the K. and P. when the road was young. One of the Beans, Charles, an attorney, was one of the most eccentric characters in Upstate New York.

Charley Bean conducted a mythical Endymion Academy

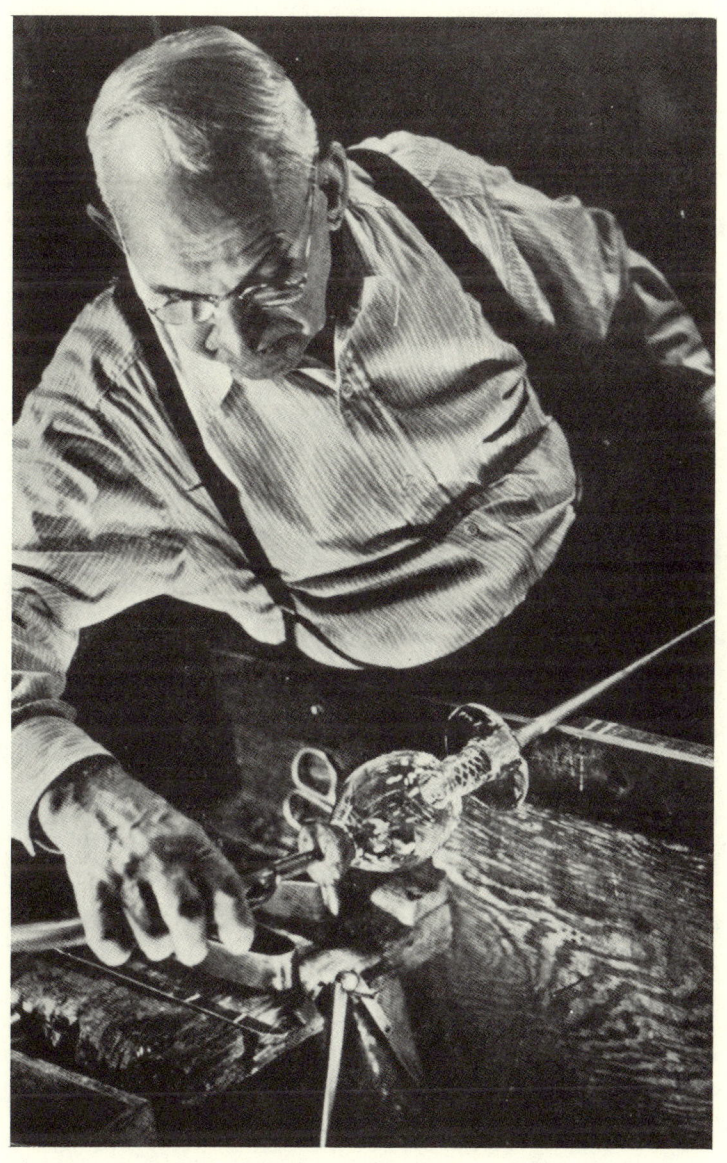

Craftsman in Crystal at Corning

Biggest Piece of Glass Ever Cast, on Exhibit at Corning Glass Center

in a barn of the present Lafayette Inn near Geneva. He sent out circulars, describing its "curriculum" and even printed some beautifully embossed diplomas. Bean, a cultivated and widely traveled man, met the great actress, Sarah Bernhardt, on one of his trips abroad.

On his return there arose on his farm along the Bath-Prattsburg road a curious monument, a pillar of concrete blocks, about six feet square and eight feet tall. It is still there, although this inscription upon it has faded a bit with the years:

To Madame Sarah Bernhardt
The Greatest Actress on Earth, whose Lyric Fire and Divine
Voice gave more Intense and Supreme Life to the Poets.
In profound admiration is built this rugged Memorial by
The Knights of Cypress and Devoted Friends.

Who were the Knights of Cypress? They, like Endymion Academy, existed only in the vivid imagination of Charley Bean.

Chapter 22

Of Wine and Wings

The visitor to the vineyard country in old Steuben's northeastern corner can get a heady feeling without imbibing any of its celebrated champagne. The sheer grandeur of the landscape around Lake Keuka's southern shores produces the same effect.

Hammondsport, at the head of the two-pronged Finger Lake, is the wine capital of the East. Its setting is magnificent. It is ringed by towering hills and Keuka's azure radiance. This Southern Tier village has a charm, a way of life and a history that is all its own.

It has been called "The Cradle of Aviation," as well as "The Grape Bowl." It was in this countryside, in the early years of the century, a native son, Glenn Hammond Curtiss, built and flew some of America's first flying machines. His pioneering has put his name next to the Wright brothers in aviation's roll of honor.

Jim Smellie, the druggist, summed up his home town, which has a population of about 1,200, in these words:

"This is the biggest little town in the state. You see, we've had the wineries and we've had Curtiss. We have seen some mighty important events and some pretty big people here. Hammondsport may not impress strangers. On the other hand, few strangers can impress Hammondsport."

Not that Hammondsport is haughty. Urbane is the word for the wine capital in the Town of Urbana.

The village gets its name from Lazarus Hammond, who in 1807 laid out its streets and public square. When the Crooked Lake Canal, linking Keuka and Seneca Lakes, was completed in 1830, Hammondsport became a booming port. Its settlers dreamed of a metropolis at the head of what they called "The Crooked Lake," because of Keuka's irregular outline. But the advent of the Erie Railroad doomed the canal and shattered the dream.

The mighty Keuka grape industry had its roots in the garden of an Episcopal clergyman. Around 1840 the Rev. William Bostwick planted some slips of the Isabella and Catawba vines in the garden of the rectory at Hammondsport. They flourished in the saintly soil. Others more commercially minded than the good rector began planting vineyards and shipping grapes to Eastern markets.

In 1860 the French vintner, Charles D. Champlin, came to aptly-named Pleasant Valley, south of Hammondsport. He found there a parallel to the famous grape country around Rheims, France. There were the same advantageous climate, soil and drainage, the same abundance of sunshine, minimum of insects and fungi. Besides, the hills provided a natural shelter and the frosts came late.

In 1861 Champlin established the first winery in the area. The Pleasant Valley Wine Company, the present name of the company he founded, still holds U. S. winery license No. 1. For years its postoffice address was Rheims, N. Y.

The Urbana Wine Company began business in 1865. It is still operating. Urbana, Pleasant Valley, Taylor Brothers, founded in 1880, and a relative newcomer D. W. Putnam, comprise the Big Four of the industry.

The industry thrived after the Civil War. By the late 1890s there were 25,000 acres of vineyards in "The American Rhineland" around Keuka Lake. In those days steamboats and tow barges hauled the grapes down the lake and sometimes six freight trains a day ran out of Hammondsport on the 9-mile-long Bath & Hammondsport Railroad.

The motor truck changed all that. The steamboats are only memory but the little railroad is still in operation. Its principal cargo is wine and its red cabooses are labeled "The Champagne Route." The B. & H. began in 1875 and was narrow gauge until about 1890. Once four passenger trains ran daily each way and there were many excursions from Rochester, Elmira, Corning and other places, in those halcyon days when the fare included a steamboat ride on Lake Keuka and a visit to the wine cellars.

In the depression year of 1935, a small group of local business men took over the short line. They still operate it. Winemaker Putnam is its president. One freight train is operated daily to Bath, where there is a connection with the Erie. The road has one steam locomotive and a diesel-electric engine.

U. S. Arland, vice president of the B. & H., handed me a card, an honorary pass on the "Champagne Route," which stated, among other things, that "a short line is a hell of a lot better than no line" and that "it is not as long as the others but just as wide."

The grape harvest in the Fall is a stupendous affair. Armies of men and women go out into the vineyards to cut the clusters from the vines with knives and shears and put the grapes, the Elviras, the Isabellas, the Delawares, the Catawbas, the Concords, into boxes to be trucked to the wineries.

The wine cellars are fascinating places. Some of the massive stone structures are built into the hillsides in the Old World fashion. There you see the jolly vintners, their white frocks stained a gaudy purple, the cool, vaulted cellars with miles of tube carrying the crimson liquid, the huge storage tanks, the rows of bottles on the racks.

This Keuka corner is not like the rest of the Southern Tier. The wine industry breeds a warm and open handed way of life. It also has given the Keuka area a sound and stable economy—since the repeal of the Eighteenth Amendment.

* * *

Glenn Curtiss was a thin, shy balding man who hated speech making and ceremony and was more at home tinkering with machinery than in plushy offices or at banquet tables.

When he was three years old he was found playing in the rear of his father's harness shop with some rather unusual "toys"—scraps of metal. At 17 he opened a little shop for the repair and sale of bicycles in his native village. He devised a bicycle which he called the Hercules. Then he added a motor to the bike and began making motorcycle engines. He raced his own motorcycles and won two world's records.

In 1903, the year of the Wright brothers' epochal flight on the sands of Kitty Hawk, Curtiss began making motors for balloons. Among his orders was one from the government, Uncle Sam's first timid step down the path of military aeronautics.

With Alexander Graham Bell, inventor of the telephone, and others, Curtiss carried out in Hammondsport the pioneer work of the Aerial Experimental Association. Out of that came the first airplane flight in New York State. On March 22, 1908, without any fanfare, a crate-like contraption with a single thickness of red silk covering two kite-like wings, with beams and struts of spruce and with a 24 horsepower, eight cylinder Curtiss motor, was put on the flat top of a grape-hauling barge, three miles up ice-coated Keuka Lake. With F. W. "Casey" Baldwin at the stick, the "Red Wing" actually flew 318 feet. Then it keeled over like a wounded duck.

On July 4, 1908 the slopes of Pleasant Valley were black with people. The magazine, *Scientific American,* had offered a prize to the first American to fly one kilometer (0.621 miles). Curtiss built the June Bug for the test. After waiting hours until "the wind was right," Curtiss flew the "crate" nearly a mile and the cup was his. Hammondsport was the scene of the first public, preannounced flight in America.

Curtiss' prestige soared. The little shop near his home that began in 1901 with three hands, was employing 300. Later, the June Bug was fitted with pontoons and alighted many times on Keuka Lake. That was the birth of naval aviation.

In 1909 Curtiss received the first order for an airplane ever given an American manufacturer. That same year he won the International Speed Race in Rheims, France, a place which must have reminded the lean, different American of the grape-growing countryside of his nativity. When he came back to Hammondsport, a 20-man team of his neighbors pulled his carriage through the streets under a hastily-built arch of triumph.

In 1911 Curtiss opened the first flying school in America. His students came from many lands. They dashed over the dusty roads in rakish automobiles. They danced all hours at the pavilions along the lake. There were parties at the wine magnates' mansions.

About the same time Curtiss organized his Flying Circus and to Hammondsport came such pioneer barnstorming daredevils as Lincoln Beachey, Beckwith Havens and Eugene Ely. Curtiss built flying boats and rich sportsmen like William Thaw and Harold McCormick came, took lessons and bought planes.

The eyes of the world were upon little Hammondsport in 1914. The pioneer Langley plane, symbol of a great defeat, was brought from Washington to be reconditioned and flown in a scientific demonstration that stirred much controversy.

That same year Curtiss built a flying boat, the America, for Rodman Wanamaker and newspapermen from the big cities flocked to little Hammondsport to report its progress. The flying boat never spanned the Atlantic as planned, because the world went to war about the time it was to take off from Newfoundland.

The war brought an immediate boom to Hammondsport. Curtiss was just developing his famous tractor biplane, the J.N., better known as "Jenny," in which so many World War I flyers were trained. Curtiss bought and built large factories in Buffalo and the Hammondsport plant roared day and night.

The Armistice ended the aviation boom. Curtiss had made a fortune. In addition to his other accomplishments, he had trained the first mail flyers, demonstrated bombing from aircraft, the sending and receiving of wireless in flight and sharpshooting from a moving plane.

Glenn Curtiss died in Buffalo in 1930 after an operation for appendicitis. His funeral was the biggest Hammondsport had ever known. Noted aviators, industrialists, government officials mingled with the villagers and farm folk who had watched the local boy who could fix door bells and bicycles rise to the pinnacle of fame.

His homestead still stands on the hill, moved back a bit to make way for the Curtiss Memorial School on the site of the old aircraft factory. It houses the school's home service department.

A handful of oldtimers who worked with Curtiss still live in the region. One is Henry Klecker, once called by Curtiss, "the greatest mechanic I have ever known." Klecker runs a garage in Bath and travels around in an ancient car with an acetylene tank on its side. He helped Curtiss design the engines that won the flyer fame. Henry's motto was "I fix 'em." Still living in Hammondsport is William E. "Gink" Doherty, who flew the reconditioned Langley plane over Lake Keuka.

Aircraft parts are still being made in Hammondsport—by the Mercury Aircraft Corporation which employs some 400 hands. Most of its present production is metal parts for International Business Machines.

For years there's been talk of some sort of memorial to Glenn Curtiss in his home town. So far it has been a dream that has not been realized. But would Glenn Curtiss, who all his busy life dealt with swiftly moving things, care for a monument or some other stationary memorial? Every airplane that roars through the skies today is in a sense a memorial to that pioneer of flying pioneers.

* * *

The shores of Keuka Lake are lined with Summer homes. People from Elmira, Corning and other nearby places come to Keuka in the good old Summertime.

Those shores also are haunted by memories—of the steamboats that once plied the Y-shaped lake, with grapes and other produce in their holds and passengers in shirt waists and straw "skimmers" on their decks, of the moonlight excursions when the band played "Sweet Marie" and "Red Wing."

It has been many a Summer since a steamboat has docked at Grove Springs, Gibson Landing, Keuka, Urbana, Hammondsport or any other of the old ports. The steamboats are only memories now in gray heads—the Yates, the Lulu, the Urbana, the Farley Holmes, the Halsey, the West Branch and the last of the lake fleet, the proud Mary Bell, the all steel screw steamer that tied up for the last time in 1922.

Still on the scene but no longer catering to the steamboat trade is the gracious old Keuka Hotel, opposite Bluff Point, the towering headland that guards the joining of the two branches of the Crooked Lake—one of the scenic highlights of the Finger Lakes Country. In that old hotel thousands have danced the nights away. Among the college musicians who played in the orchestras of yesteryear were Fred Waring and Hoagy Carmichael, then unknown to fame.

Perched above the west fork of Keuka Lake, Pulteney village drowses amid the vineyards. There, according to a widely-accepted tradition in the countryside, the world's first jinrikisha was fashioned, the forerunner of thousands of the man-drawn carts that have rumbled down the streets of the Orient.

In 1859, so the story goes, Keuka-born Jonathan Goble, a Baptist missionary in Japan, conceived the idea of a two-wheeled cart in which he could transport his ailing wife, Eliza, through the streets of Yokohama.

Goble remembered a former shipmate, Frank Pollay, who was a wagonmaker in Pulteney. He had served with Pollay on Commodore Perry's historic cruise to Japan which in 1853 opened the island kingdom to the western world. The missionary wrote to his wagonmaker friend, asking him to devise a cart to be hauled by a man between the shafts.

There are conflicting stories as to whether Pollay actually

made the parts and shipped them to Japan or merely sent the patterns of the vehicle to Goble. There seems to be little question that the world's first jinrikisha was the technical brain child of the wagonmaker who sleeps in Pulteney burying ground.

"The Big House" is off the beaten path and the average tourist never sees the abandoned mansion on the hill with its 24 massive pillars, in the Town of Wayne, just over the Schuyler County line and on the Wayne-Hammondsport road.

For a quarter of a century now "The Big House," as it is called in the neighborhood, has been vacant and vandals and the elements have done their worst, but about it still hangs an aura of past glory.

Its first occupant, Canisteo-born Samuel Hallett, the railroad builder, called it "Lake Home." Hallett had just completed the first section of the Union Pacific Railroad when he was shot to death on the streets of Wyandotte, Kansas, in 1864. His widow became a recluse and because of her strange ways, the place was called "haunted."

Then in the early 1900s, George K. Birge, the Buffalo Pierce-Arrow automobile tycoon, leased the estate and made extensive improvements, even moving the mansion back on the hill. He renamed it the "Aisle of Pines" because of the rows of tall trees that line its walks and driveways. After Birge's death in 1918, the place was unoccupied. It currently is owned by an Elmira priest.

It is magnificent, even in desolation and decay. Few traces remain of the private race track, the sunken garden, the swimming pool. The brambles and weeds are taking over the spacious grounds, the once trim lawns and gardens. But the private cemetery of the Halletts is untouched and the view from the roof walk of three lakes, Keuka, Waneta and Lamoka, is as splendid as in the days when lights shone from its tall windows, when logs blazed in the fireplaces and Hallett carriages and Birge Pierce-Arrows rolled up under its now sagging porte-cochere.

Chapter 23

Bath, the Grand Dame

Visiting Bath is like turning the pages of a rare old book. There is almost the air of a capital city about this old town on the Conhocton although its population is less than 6,000 and it is the seat of government merely of the County of Steuben. At that it has to share its court terms with Hornell and Corning.

Streets, broad and straight and laid out according to an orderly plan, tell even the casual visitor that long ago some bold dreamer planned a city in this broad valley over which great hills with shaggy leonine heads stand watch.

The stately square in the village's heart, flanked by timeworn, buff-colored county buildings and mansions with pillars, whispers of a distinguished past. To me Bath has always been "The Grand Dame" of the Southern Tier.

During the feverish days of land speculation in the wake of the Revolution, Bath was born in the busy brain of the greatest real estate salesman of his time. Scottish-born Charles Williamson, agent for the British Pulteney interests, with a million wilderness acres to sell and to settle, was a former soldier of the crown, an enterprising, daring man with the superb optimism of the born promoter. And he had a charm that few men—or women—could resist.

No man played a stronger role in Western New York's early years. Williamson founded towns, built highways and schools, staged fairs and races to advertise the glories of his wilderness "empire," dreamed and schemed and toiled. He accomplished much in a brief seven years.

From the first he picked the basin of the Conhocton as the center of his far-flung enterprises. He saw in his mind's eyes the commerce of the frontier floating down the Conhocton, the Chemung, the Tioga to the Susquehanna and the great port of Baltimore. In 1793 he could not foresee the coming of the Erie Canal to cut a shorter outlet to the sea and to make New York the commercial mistress of the western world.

At the junction of his land and water highways the land agent envisioned a trading and manufacturing center, in the heart of a rich farm country which he would call Bath after the famous English watering place, the seat of his principal, Sir William Pulteney.

Williamson did things with celerity and on a grand scale. His axemen, commanded by the scout and Indian fighter, Benjamin Patterson, first blazed a trail over the mountains from Lycoming Creek in the State of Penn to the Painted Post.

Then his men in the Spring of 1793 came poling their Durham boats up the winding, log-strewn Conhocton and sprang ashore to make the first clearing at the present site of Pulteney Square.

Quickly a settlement arose around that cradle of the frontier—the land office, the agent's house, a tavern and a huddle of cabins. Then came grist and saw mills and the first newspaper in the backwoods. Williamson even built a theater on the square. And it presented the sophisticated comedies of Moliere. When a new county was formed, the land agent saw to it that his town of Bath, the pride of his heart, was made the shire town.

He built the finest residence on the frontier, a frame

mansion with wings and porches and elaborate gardens, beside a sparkling lake which he called Salubra. The hospitality, choice viands and wines of Springfield Farms became famous. There the petulant Abigail, the Boston girl who had married the British captain when he was a prisoner of war, played hostess. Celebrated guests came, among them Louis Philippe, later a king of France; the Duke de Liancourt and other titled travelers, and the scheming Aaron Burr.

In 1795 as a promotion stunt to lure land buyers, Williamson laid out a race course at Bath and announced a fair, racing meet, barbecue and wrestling matches on a scale unheard of on any frontier.

He sent out couriers in all directions with handbills which proclaimed: "There will be trusty and civil guides to meet and conduct gentlemen and their suites to the far-famed city on the upper reaches of the Susquehanna, in the land of crystal lakes and memorial parks, located in the garden home of the lately vanquished Iroquois."

"Charles the Magnificent" was something of an advertising copywriter as well as a promoter.

In August of 1795 caravans rolled into Bath from all sides. Plantation owners with their Negroes, gamesters, jockeys, hunters, backwoodsmen, Indians, society ladies, pioneer women with calloused hands, to the number of 2,000, gathered on the Pine Plains of Bath, awaiting the starting gun.

There were no pari-mutuel windows but large sums changed hands. Williamson's Southern mare, Virginia Nell, raced Sheriff Dunn's New Jersey Silk Stocking, and lost. The wives of the two owners wagered $100 and a pipe of wine on the result and dumped the gold coins into the apron of a third lady who was stakeholder.

There was a sprinkling of New Englanders among the Southerners, Scots, New Jersey and Pennsylvania pioneers and Mohawk Valley Dutch who had settled in the region and they looked askance at the racing and the betting, the revelry in the tavern, the new theater and other gay goings-on in Bath.

Jemima Wilkinson, the Universal Friend, ruler of a fanatical religious colony near the Crooked Lake, regarded Bath as a den of the devil. But she and her followers had no qualms about doing a profitable business with the worldly land agent.

Williamson, reared among patricians, desired aristocratic settlers and leaned toward Southern gentry. It was through his promotions that the Rochesters, Fitzhughs, Carrolls and others came to the Genesee Country. But in the end he was selling most of his lands to impecunious followers of Tom Jefferson, men who put up liberty poles in the squares and pulled the forelock to no squire.

By 1796 Bath had 800 people. Ben Patterson was supplying 100 deer a month for the populace. From the boom town on the Conhocton raft-like arks carried timber and other products down the rivers to Baltimore—when the water was high enough.

Troubles beset the dashing land agent. Bath had the invasion jitters in 1794 when a British-Indian alliance threatened. A stockade was built and the militia drilled in Pulteney Square. But "Mad Anthony" Wayne's victory over the Indians in Ohio restored calm.

The "Genesee Fever" struck at the log houses and laid even the vigorous Williamson low. His daughter, Christian, died in 1793 at the age of 8 and her grave was the first dug in the new settlement. She sleeps in the old Presbyterian cemetery in the heart of Bath, at Steuben and Howell Streets, a little corner of the long ago amid the modern bustle.

The captain walked the primrose path and 'twas said

that in each of his mansions, at Bath, at Bluff Point above the Crooked Lake, and in Geneva, there was a woman not his wife. He and Abigail became estranged.

Williamson's greatest cross was his financial worries. He fell into disfavor with his home office when his books showed that after seven years, he had spent 185,000 pounds on developing a tract which had been bought for 75,000 pounds. His talents were mostly in the promotion field. In the end he was fired because he spent too much. And he was born a Scot!

In 1801 the more practical Robert Troup, a self-made American, succeeded him as land agent and Williamson left his "garden home." He died of yellow fever in 1806 aboard a ship bound for the West Indies.

In fancy one today can look up the broad street called Liberty toward the Pulteney Square with its backdrop of green and towering hill, and see again a gallant figure on horseback, a tall, courtly man in a blue cloak, a tricorn hat and powdered wig. His "city in the land of crystal lakes" never became the metropolis of his dreams. It did grow into a handsome county seat town, an important trading center, a distinctive community with its own mellow traditions and gracious, serene way of life. Bath still bears the imprint of its founder, "Charles the Magnificent."

The early returns from the vast tract which they had purchased in 1791 from Robert Morris at 28 cents an acre may have been disappointing to the British speculators. But the Pulteney Estate kept some of its New York State holdings a long time. It was not until 1914 that its affairs were closed out. In 1916 the old land office in Bath was torn down. It seems a pity the historic building was not preserved.

But many papers of the Pulteney Estate have been preserved. They are in the ponderous safe in the office of the

Steuben County Clerk. For 30 years Reuben B. Oldfield has held that office. He is an authority on local history and the author of eight books for children. About everybody in the county knows "Barney" Oldfield—and votes for him. He is a gentleman of the old school and his talk, always sparkling, is punctuated with infectious chuckles.

Many of the papers in the County Clerk's safe are sheepskin parchments, written in the finest copperplate. Some have scalloped edges. The torn pieces had been given as "receipts" to pioneers who could not read or write but who could match pieces of torn parchment.

Among the documents is the deed of the Pulteney lands from Robert Morris to Williamson. The property first was in Williamson's name because he was a naturalized American and his British principals could not hold legal title. The 11-page will of Henrietta Laura, Countess of Bath, and the daughter of Sir William Pulteney, is 29 inches square and gay with red ribbon and seals of wax.

Some of the Southern settlers brought along their slaves. One, William Helms of Virginia, had 50 Negroes but most of them ran away. Some of the descendants of those early slaves still live in the area.

Bath was the home of George McClure, land owner, Indian trader, mill and ship owner, general and probably Western New York's first chain store proprietor. At one time had stores in Bath, Dansville, Penn Yan and Honeoye. His military career was hardly glorious. As a general of militia in the War of 1812 it was he who evacuated Fort Niagara and opened the way for the burning of Buffalo by the British.

Then there was John Magee, the farm boy who became stage coach magnate and railroad builder. His former residence is now the Bath Library and he had running water piped under the river to his mansion.

Bath was always noted for its elegance—in the Williamson tradition. The oldtime merchants of the village would be driven to their stores in their carriages, gloved and tophatted, and they never deigned to wait on the trade but received their customers as if at a levee. And when the Erie ran special trains to the grand balls in Bath, carpeting was laid from the curb to the scene of the festivity.

But no community can thrive on elegance alone. Bath is the trading center for some 25,000 people. Around it is a prosperous farm region, noted for its dairy herds. Nearby are pleasant villages, among them Kanona, to the north, and Savona, to the south.

Kanona, an Indian name meaning "rusty water," once was Kennedyville and an important port. There coastwise vessels were built and floated down the rivers to be sold in Baltimore. After Keuka and Seneca Lakes were connected by the Crooked Lake Canal and Hammondsport was a thriving port, drovers would stop overnight in Kanona's two big hotels that they might be in Hammondsport at crack of dawn.

Savona on Mud Creek and the road to Corning has some fine old post Colonial homes, among them the stately white house where lived until his death in 1953 Alfred Spencer, student of history, and which houses the Steuben Historical Society's collection of historic relics.

For 75 years, Bath has been the site of the State Soldiers and Sailors Home, now a United States Veterans Administration Center. The home, which Bath obtained by raising $23,000 by popular subscription, more than any rival could offer, was formally opened on Christmas Day of 1878 when 25 Boys in Blue sat down to their holiday repast.

The home's population peak was reached in 1907 when it had 2,143 residents, most of them veterans of the Civil War. In those days blue was the dominant color on the streets of Bath when the old soldiers in forage caps or broad brimmed hats, in gold braid and brass buttons came downtown and drivers of the horse-drawn hacks vied for their custom, at 10 cents the ride. Now the "boys from the hill" wear no distinctive garb. Many of them walk with canes—and not to be stylish.

The population sank to its lowest point in 1928 with only 192 residents. Then the veterans of the first World War began to pour in.

In 1930 the federal government took over the state institution. Now the home-hospital on the banks of the Conhocton at the edge of Bath is a full-fledged government VA Center.

The first shovel of earth for a million-dollar, 430-bed hospital was turned in 1936 by the trembling hand of a 97-year-old veteran of the Civil War, who was taken to the scene in a wheel chair. Since then a fireproof dormitory barrack, a store house, a canteen-cafeteria and a new sewage disposal plant have been built. But the first unit, that was considered grand when it was built in 1878, still serves, along with three other barracks over 65 years old, with high-ceilinged rooms, supported by interior pillars.

The institution as of mid June, 1953, housed 1,650 veterans of four wars. Of that number 1,345 are "members," as those at the home are called. All who are physically able are assigned to duties. The hospital has 305 patients. In the center are 56 veterans of the War with Spain; 1,382 of World War I; 172 of World War II; nine of the Korean conflict and 29 listed as "miscellaneous."

They come from many states but principally from New York and Pennsylvania. They are of all faiths and races, with many Negroes among them. The home's family has included doctors, lawyers, scientists—and some newspapermen.

The manager since shortly after the close of the second World War is a brisk veteran of both world conflicts, Col. John I. Spreckelmyer. He runs a veritable "city," with a population nearly a third as large as that of Bath. An institution with a staff of 600 has a payroll that means something to the village economy.

Bath never was an industrial community—until lately. It has had for years the Babcock ladder factory, which used to make churns. It also has the Lane Pipe Company.

Now there is a new, modern and sprawling plant on the edge of town, along the road to Hammondsport. It is an electronics tube unit of the giant Westinghouse Company. Eventually it is scheduled to employ 2,000 to 3,000 people. An industry of that size is bound to have an impact on a community of less than 6,000.

Industry, with mass production and union labor, is something new to the old county seat-trading center. It is bound to change the village. But any change will be superficial.

For I do not believe anything can alter the basic character of this stately and historic village, amid great green hills, Charles Williamson's old town with its two shady public squares, its signs at its gates that say "Welcome to Bath," its row of electric lights in the center of the mall of one of its leading thoroughfares, its air of consequence and above its sure serenity.

Bath will always be "The Grand Dame of the Southern Tier."

Chapter 24

Indomitable Hornell

Gallant is the word for Hornell. It has an indomitable spirit, this old railroad town, this Maple City of 15,000 that spills out of the Canisteo Valley to climb the steep Steuben hillsides.

Hornell has "met with triumph and disaster" and "treated those two impostors just the same," to borrow some lines from Kipling.

It has felt the devastating wrath of the flood waters roaring down from the hills on its vulnerable heart in the lowlands. It cleared up the mess and tamed the rampaging rivers.

It has known economic heights and depths. For a century its fortunes have been closely linked with the destinies of the Erie Railroad. The first wood burner that crawled over the hills of the Southern Tier in 1851 unfurled the smoky banner that has been the symbol of its prosperity. A century later the diesel engine glided into dominance and a pall fell over that bulwark of the city's economy, the sprawling Erie car shops where for years the iron horses had been groomed. Hornell is rallying from that economic body blow—with its old spirit.

Hornell is still a railroad town, an important cog in the Erie system. It still has the railroad's division storehouse and accounting bureau and it is a busy freight transfer point. And the car shops are by no means idle. But only a handful of electricians are needed to repair diesels where hundreds used to mend the steam locomotives in the 27 great bays in the Erie shops.

The Maple City has several lively industries. It has been a textile center for a long time. Some of its plants are newcomers and a live Board of Trade is constantly gunning for more.

It is the trading area for an estimated 75,000 people. Its retail shopping district is impressive. It claims to have the largest department store in the Southern Tier. Its business does not straggle along a single street. There are three busy central thoroughfares. Hornell looks like a city.

* * *

The first white settler was Benjamin Crosby who in 1790 cleared the present site of St. James Mercy Hospital. His nearest neighbor was an Indian named Straight Back who lived near the present Seneca Street bridge. About them hangs a little tale. It seems Crosby invited Straight Back to dinner and served the meal in courses. The Indian returned the invitation and in his home the meal also was in courses—each of the same dish, succotash.

The settlement was first known as Upper Canisteo because it was on the old Indian river of that name. The present village of Canisteo was called Lower Canisteo.

Upper Canisteo became Hornell, after the arrival of George Hornell, an Indian trader, in 1792, to settle on the several thousand acres he had bought. He brought a number of slaves. Hornell set up grist mills, opened the first store and inn and became a judge. It was logical the settlement should bear his name. It was Hornellsville until 1906.

Lumbering was an important pioneer industry and the great ark-rafts carried, not only lumber, but also cattle, cheese and wheat to Baltimore. The first ark went down the river in 1800 from the village north of Hornell that ever since has been Arkport. The pioneer ark owner was Judge Christopher Hurlbut whose home, built 148 years ago, still stands in Arkport, the village surrounded by rich mucklands.

The advance guard of the Erie Railroad, which was to mean so much to Hornell, appeared in 1841 in the form of a machine which was a combination pile driver, steam locomotive and a saw mill. It moved on wheels, drove two piles at a time and sawed them off at the level as it passed.

The first Erie train puffed into Hornellsville in September, 1850. It was hauled by the famous little old Orange No. 4, the trail-blazer for the Erie, which had won a 20-mile race with a stage coach.

Hornellsville was gay with flags when the first train to traverse the entire length of the Erie steamed into town on May 16, 1851, with President Fillmore, Daniel Webster and other notables aboard. After the usual cheers, oratory, music, dining and toasts, the train changed engines and resumed its triumphal tour. It was the first of thousands of trains to change engines in Hornell.

Even before the road was completed, the first car shops were built, in 1849. The next year they were enlarged. When in 1852 Hornellsville became the southern terminus of a branch line to Buffalo, the village began to boom mightily and fortunes were made in real estate.

The first car shops burned in 1856. But larger shops already were under construction at the time and the new plant was dedicated with a grand ball later in the year. After 1928 and until the diesel took over in the mid Twentieth Century, all the heavy repair work of the Erie system was concentrated in the Hornell shops.

For a century the theme song of Hornell has been "I've Been Working on the Railroad." The Iron Horse gave the town life and color. Now Loder Street is not so gaudy as of yore and there are fewer grog shops facing the old red station and the maze of tracks.

Hornell was the scene of a serious labor disturbance in 1877. A 10 per cent wage cut brought a strike in the Erie yards. After switches had been spiked and tracks torn up by unruly mobs, the militia was called out to patrol the yards. Among the troops sent to Hornell were the men of Rochester's 54th Regiment. Their blue uniforms awed the strikers who thought the 54th was a regular army outfit.

For years Hornell was a terminus of the now defunct Shawmut Railroad. When Mrs. Clara Higgins Smith, widow of the former Shawmut president, died in New York some 30 years ago, she willed half of her six million dollar estate to the American Red Cross. The bequest included the 10-mile Shawmut branch from Hornell to Moraine Park, once an amusement resort, now an Elks recreation park. The Red Cross, which did not particularly care to go into the railroad business, sold the branch to the Erie.

For a long time Hornell has been a silk and cloth-making center. The Merrill silk mill, which began in 1890 and once was a big glove manufacturer, now makes silk hosiery. Also in that field is the Huguet Division of Stern & Stern Textiles, an important industry, as is a relative newcomer, American Hardware, which makes postal equipment and employs 200.

Other Hornell industries include Forbes & Wagner, electronics; Chapman Transmission; a branch of the Hickey-Freeman Company, Rochester clothing manufacturers; a dress shop and a brewery.

The big layoff in the Erie shops after dieselization at first caused consternation. But most of the boiler makers, steamfitters and other mechanics have kept their homes in Hornell. Many of them have found jobs in other communities. Throughout the Southern Tier there is a cross current of traffic in the morning and at night. So many people live in Hornell and work in Dansville or Wayland or live in Bath and work in Corning and vice-versa. The housing shortage is largely responsible.

Hornell's mayor is Francis P. Hogan, who is something of an economist as well as a politician. A former executive in the textile industry, he has acted vigorously to take up the economic slack caused by the car shop layoffs. He set up the office of industrial commissioner, whose job it is to keep the city's present industries and get new ones. Hornell's commissioner, Robert Kohnke, works closely with the Board of Trade which shares the expenses of his office with the municipality.

Four streams pour down the rough, steep hills to join the main waterway in the valley, the Canisteo River. They are the Canacadea, Crosby Creek, Chancey Run and Big Creek. Swollen by rains or thaws, these generally demure streams become raging torrents. From its beginning Hornell in its vulnerable basin has been plagued with floods.

The flood of floods struck in 1935. On Sunday, June 7, a cloudburst smote the Southern Tier and parts of the Finger Lakes region. Morning found two thirds of Hornell under water, 6 feet high in places. Two persons were drowned. Property damage was enormous. Hundreds of families were marooned and boats patroled the streets. Highways were blocked and the main line of the Erie was under five feet of water. Water mains were broken, causing a serious health hazard. At night the city was in darkness.

Hornell was a stricken, isolated city, hardest hit of many in the state. Its mayor appealed for food and clothing for the homeless, for whom public buildings were thrown open for shelter. Martial law was declared and National Guardsmen from all over Western New York took over the city of wrecked buildings and yellow mud. The Red Cross and other relief agencies went into action and 1,000 refugees were cared for. Governor Lehman and other officials came to inspect the disaster scene. Gradually Hornell emerged from the slime of its greatest flood.

Since then two huge earthen flood control dams have been built by the federal government, one near Arkport and another at Almond. The streams that course through the city have been deepened and widened and retaining walls have been built. In all more than seven million dollars were spent on flood control in the vicinity. That sum approximates the estimated damage caused by the big flood of 1935.

Already these measures have proved their worth. Hornell has escaped when recent floods swept "The Tier."

Here are some Maple City sidelights:

Big Ed (Porky) Oliver, one of the nation's golfing stars, in the early 1940s was the "pro" at the Country Club in North Hornell.

Chauncey Olcott, the great Irish singer, in his youth tended bar in a Hornell saloon. Oldtimers vouch for that.

Mrs. Mary Karr Jackson is one of the two women city judges in the state.

James E. Swartzenbach was a prominent brewer in the city. The road from Hornell to Wayland via Haskinville is called the Swartzenbach Highway. Along it is a stone fountain, a memorial to the brewer erected by his friends in 1925. From it gushes clear, cold spring water.

Hornell claims to have established in 1868 the first village library in Western New York.

* * *

It is hard to believe that Canisteo, attractive village amid the green hills south of Hornell, once was an outlaw stronghold.

There in the 17th and 18th centuries lived a motley band of the lawless of all races, Indians of many tribes, renegade Frenchmen, rascally Dutchmen, Yankee fugitives from justice, runaway Negro slaves. They cleared enough land in the lush valley to build some 60 houses.

The French in 1690 sent an expedition under Sieur de Villiers to "Kanisteo Castle." The outlaws fled at the approach of the invaders, who after unfurling the flag of France and celebrating Mass, departed.

The outcasts soon returned to their old base. British Army deserters joined them and two forts were built to protect the "castle." In 1786 two Dutch traders, subjects of England, were waylaid and slain there. Two years later Sir William Johnson, lord of the Mohawk Valley, sent a party of 140 men under the half breed, Captain Andrew Montour, to destroy the wilderness vipers' nest. Again the occupants fled and this time the invaders burned the houses, killed the livestock and blotted out the outlaw refuge.

In 1788 Solomon Bennett, John Jameson, Uriah Stephens and Richard Crosby came from Pennsylvania and "discovered" the fair Canisteo Valley. They formed a pool of 12 men, some of them survivors of the Wyoming, Pa., Indian massacre, and bought a tract from Phelps and Gorham.

The next year settlement began at "Lower Canisteo." It was a wild place and stage drivers would whip up their horses and dash through the unruly town. They could not tell what deviltry "the Canisteers" would be up to.

Chapter 25

The Painted Post

The Painted Post was there before ever a white man came to the old Indian valley.

The massive hand-hewn marker of oak stood where the Tioga and Conhocton Rivers join to form the Chemung and where the Indian trails forked. It was a landmark, a rendezvous in the wilderness empire of the Six Nations.

Its origin is shrouded in legend. No man knows for sure who put it there or why or when. There are conflicting stories.

General Freegift Patchen, a prisoner of the Mohawk war chief, Joseph Brant, in 1780, has left this narrative:

"An Indian chief on this spot had been victorious in battle, killed and took prisoners to the number of about 60. This event he celebrated by causing a tree to be taken from the forest and hewed four square, painted red, and the number he killed, which was 28, represented across the post in black paint, without any heads. But those he took prisoner, which were 30, were represented in black paint, with their heads on. This post he erected and thus handed down to posterity an account that here a battle was fought but by whom and who the sufferers were is covered in darkness, except that it was between whites and Indians."

Another version has the post erected to mark the grave of Andrew Montour, one of a famous Indian family in whose veins coursed proud French blood. Montour, so the story goes, was brought there to die after he had been wounded in a border skirmish along the west branch of the Susquehanna in 1779.

Benjamin Gilbert, who had seen the Painted Post as a captive of the Indians during the Revolution, described it thus in 1785:

"At a central crossroads of the principal Indian trails and a general resting place for the Indians . . . a huge post had been set up in an open place and painted in fantastic manner. When war parties halted at this place, they usually held 'brag dances' about the post."

Another pioneer, Samuel Cook, gave this description of the landmark in 1792: "It was an oak post 10 to 12 feet above the ground and from 10 to 14 inches square. It was square to a height of four feet above ground and then octagonal to the top. At that time it had no marks or carving on it and was the color of a weather-beaten oak rail."

The Painted Post was there when in 1784 the first white settlers, Samuel Harris and his son, William, Pennsylvanians, hunters and Indian traders, built a log cabin on the river near the marker. It was at the Harris cabin that the surveyors of the Phelps and Gorham Purchase made their headquarters in 1789.

In the Spring of 1790 Colonel Eleazer Lindsley of Morristown, N. J., a veteran of the Revolution, brought up the rivers on flatboats 37 people, who made the first permanent settlement in the county, along the slope of a hill overlooking the bottom lands of the Tioga River, south of the Painted Post. It was on the tract Colonel Lindsley had bought, including the township which today bears his name, corrupted to Lindley.

That same year another soldier of the Revolution, British-born Colonel Arthur Erwin, on his way from his home in

Erwin, Pa. to Canandaigua with a herd of beef cattle, stopped at the Painted Post. He was struck by the rich promise of the river valleys and bought and settled the township which still bears his name. He was mysteriously murdered but his two sons carried out his plans for settlement.

When the Winter of 1790-91 set in, there were three settlements in what became known as "The District of the Painted Post," the little colony at Lindley's; 25 settlers at Erwin's; 59 at the site of Corning, then without a name, besides a few scattered homes on the Upper Canisteo and the cabins of squatters and woodsmen.

After the County of Steuben was established in 1796, the town of Painted Post was set up, embracing the present townships of Erwin, Lindley, Corning, Campbell, Hornby and Caton. The term "District of the Painted Post" ceased to exist.

But the name lives on to this day—in the industrial village that grew up around the place where the rivers and trails met. Today tourists, knowing nothing of its history, are likely to exclaim: "Painted Post, what an odd name."

And save for brief intervals there has stood in the heart of the village a figure symbolic of its storied past. During one period there were two such symbols.

The original post, the one known to the pioneers, rotted away and in 1808 was replaced by a shaft 30 feet high. The oldtimer found a home in the log tavern of Captain Samuel Erwin until one night some roistering boatmen tossed it into the Conhocton River.

In 1824 Captain Erwin had a more permanent symbol fashioned. It was the sheet iron figure of a tribesman in head dress, jacket and leggings. For a quarter of a century this warrior swung from a pole.

Another sheet metal Indian came on the scene in 1880. It was the life-size figure of a chief in a red jacket and buckskin trousers, complete with bow and tomahawk and attached to the top of a tapered octagonal post 10 feet high and painted red. This figure stood at Water and Hamilton Streets until the 1920s.

He had a rival. In 1894, through funds raised by popular subscription, a stone memorial surmounted by the metal figure of an Indian chief, was erected in Water Street. The windstorm of November 20, 1948 toppled and shattered that brave.

In 1950 the present symbol took up his stand at the traditional site on what is now called Monument Square. This Indian of bronze stands with hand raised in welcome, atop a sturdy stone pedestal and with a tall post at his back. The village and township raised $10,000 for this monument and dedicated it with a three-day ceremonial.

The 1824 sheet metal Indian, the one toppled by the wind and the original plaster model of the present chief are housed in the Town Hall and Historical Museum in Water Street, along with other relics of Indian and pioneer times.

The village of Painted Post is the home of the largest air compressor plant in the world. The immense main factory of the Ingersoll-Rand Company sprawls over a city block in the heart of the village. Ingersoll-Rand employs nearly 2,700. The population of Painted Post is 2,405.

Lumbering was the principal industry in the early days and the first saw mill was built about 1833 at what became known as Gang Mills, south of Painted Post. Later the mills were rebuilt and operated by steam and for a time Gang Mills was the biggest lumbering establishment in Upstate New York.

In 1848 a foundry and machine shop were set up at

Painted Post and Abijah Weston, who had been a king pin in the lumber industry at Gang Mills, made engines in the plant. He sold out in 1898 to the Rand Drill Company, makers of air compressors. In 1905 Rand was consolidated with the Ingersoll-Sargeant Drill Company and out of that merger grew the mighty Ingersoll-Rand Company of today, which puts out electric, gas and diesel engines, as well as air compressors. The motors are shipped to Painted Post and assembled at the plant there.

At the historic crossroads where once the Indian trails met and where now busy Routes 15 and 17 join, industry and history merge. If you stand by the Indian in Monument Square and listen closely, you can catch the beat of tom-toms, faint and far away. That is, if you are imaginative enough.

There is nothing fanciful about the steady throb of the machinery in the world's largest air compressor factory across the way. You can hear it in any corner of the village. It is the heart beat of Painted Post.

Chapter 26

Corning, the Crystal City

Few American cities of its size (17,684) are as widely known as Corning, N. Y.

For Corning is the Crystal City, world center of the technical and art glass industry. In Corning in 1879 was made the glass bulb for Edison's first incandescent lamp. Corning products have made railroad traffic safer, have eased the lot of housewives, have advanced medical science. Exquisite crystal glassware made in Corning has graced White House and royal tables. A glass lamp made in Corning sheds a soft glow at the Holy Sepulcher in Jerusalem.

In an observatory atop a California mountain is a 20-ton, 200-inch telescope disk the largest piece of glass ever cast. That also came from Corning, N. Y.

All along the principal Eastern highways, the traveler sees the signs that bid him to "visit the Corning Glass Center, ... miles to Corning." Since it was opened in May of 1951, up to mid July of 1953, no less than 800,000 pilgrims have accepted that invitation and visited the house of magic that is the Corning Glass Center where the story of glass-making through the centuries is unfolded.

One afternoon I made a five-minute check of the license plates of the cars parked around the Corning Glass Center and found that 28 states and two foreign countries were represented.

The story of Corning is the story of glass-making. The

two are inseparable. Yet there was a community on the south bank of the Chemung before ever a piece of glass was blown there.

Corning's early history had elements of drama and Nature provided a dramatic setting for the future Crystal City. Steep and towering hills rise abruptly from the smoky valley that is pierced by the winding Chemung River and the antic stream known as the Monkey Run. The spectacle is glorious when the wooded hills are ablaze with the colors of the Autumn.

The city bears the name of Erastus Corning but that Albany magnate, one of a company of speculators that founded the town in 1835, made but one recorded visit to the community that was in future years to lend such luster to his family name. That was 1855.

How could Erastus Corning back in 1855 foresee that the struggling little lumber town on the Chemung River and the Chemung Canal would one day be the seat of an industrial colossus?

* * *

Where the Crystal City stands today once was the Munsey Indian village of Assinisink, destroyed by the British in 1764.

After the Revolution had been won and Sullivan's raid on the Indian country had opened Western New York to white settlement, the pioneers began to drift into the "District of the Painted Post."

First on the scene was a Vermont Yankee, Frederick Calkins who in 1789 built a log cabin and cleared the land along the Chemung at the place long known as the Chimney Narrows because of the three pillars of shale rock that stood there—until the advent of the Lackawanna Railroad tumbled them in 1881.

Many of the settlers came from Pennsylvania and New Jersey, as well as from Eastern New York and from New England. Most of them were farmers but many went in for lumbering in the wild new country. There were rich stands of virgin timber on the hills and the rivers were handy highways for the lumber rafts.

Settlements grew up on both sides of the Chemung but the one on the north bank, named Knoxville after a pioneer innkeeper, was by far the largest. The one on the south side was so small it had no name. Knoxville kept its name and its separate identity until 1890 when it became a part of the new city of Corning. The old division still persists in separate school districts and the familiar terms, "Northside" and "Southside."

The year 1833 brought an important event in the region's economic history. In 1832 the Chemung Canal, linking the Chemung River at Elmira with Seneca Lake, had been completed. The next year a feeder was built between Horseheads and Knoxville. This waterway provided a northern outlet for the lumber and other products of the Southern Tier and for the coal of Northern Pennsylvania. Knoxville became a busy port. The canal lasted until 1878. In its day it served its region well.

In 1835 the little settlement on the south bank of the river got a name. Erastus Corning and eight other Albany capitalists had formed a land company which bought 340 acres on the south side of the Chemung. Corning's name was given both to the land company and to the projected town.

Erastus Corning had come to Albany in his youth, a cripple with $500. When he died he was worth eight millions. He was the first president of the New York Central Railroad and he founded in the capital city a family line that has since been distinguished in business and politics. But he never got around to visit the Steuben County place which had been named after him until 1855, and that was the year the Corning Company was dissolved.

By then Corning was an established community of 3,600. It had been incorporated as a village in 1848. The company had built two business blocks and, what is more important, had in 1839 fathered a 14-mile railroad, the Corning and Blossburg. At the state border it met the tracks of the Tioga Railroad which tapped the Pennsylvania coal fields.

There was rejoicing in the village when it was learned that Corning would be on the route of the New York and Erie Railroad, that early transportation bud that was so long in blooming. But the joy soon gave way to resentment.

The Erie took possession of Erie Avenue, then the principal residential street, for its tracks, instead of using a bridge at the foot of Steuben Street. The protests of the citizens were ignored and gangs began grading Erie Avenue. A mob gathered and threatened the grading crew. The contractors called his men off the job but the next Sabbath morning Corning awoke to find the ties and rails had been laid during the night.

So Corning greeted without wild acclaim the famous special train which came through in May of 1851, bearing President Fillmore, Daniel Webster and other notables and officially opening the railroad. Reporters on the Presidential train noted the smallish crowd and lack of enthusiasm at Corning, in contrast to the tumultuous receptions in other places in the Southern Tier. One writer figured it was because Corning was Democratic and all the bigwigs on the train were Whigs. That was not the reason. Corning bitterly resented the high-handed tactics of the railroad builders.

There were other grievances. For a dozen years after the Erie was built, all its locomotives were wood burners. People and buildings along the right of way were showered with sparks from the funnel-shaped stacks. Sometimes the sparks caused fires. In the days of the wood burners, there was a woodyard at each stopping place and piles at other points for emergency use. About the only ones who felt kindly toward the Erie in those days were the farmers who had contracts for supplying wood to the railroad.

No longer do the Erie trains rattle along Erie Avenue at grade in the business district of Corning. On November 22, 1952, a ribbon was snipped and the Erie's new million dollar cutoff and its fine new station, at the end of Sycamore Street on the north side of the river near the D L & W tracks, was opened.

That followed a stupendous moving job which took eighteen months. It involved moving the 400-ton Lackawanna station across the tracks, 45 homes and even, at one point, of moving the old Chemung itself. The side of a hill was cut away and used as a fill to nudge the river over to make room for the new trackage. Eight grade crossings in the center of the city were eliminated. Only the old Erie station and a blank space in the center of Erie Avenue where the tracks used to be are left. Erie Avenue is strangely quiet now. Plans are afoot to convert the old right of way into an arterial highway.

It took 101 years but Corning finally got rid of those Erie tracks in its heart.

* * *

October 22, 1868 is an epochal date in Corning history. That was the day the Corning Flint Glass Works began operations, in a new plant along the river, and with only one chimney.

It is necessary now to backtrack a bit in time, to 1851,

when a energetic Yankee, the first Amory Houghton, sold his wharf business at Somerville, Mass. and opened a glass factory there, under the name of the Union Glass Company. In 1864 he moved his business to Brooklyn where he established the Brooklyn Flint Glass Works.

In May of 1868 he moved again, shipping his equipment by canal boat to the little village of Corning in York State's Southern Tier. There he had found coal and other materials cheap and handy. There also were excellent shipping facilities by railroad and canal. Local citizens were ready to invest in the new enterprise, raising $50,000 of the $125,000 needed to start the new company, which took the name, Corning Flint Glass Works, and elected Amory Houghton its first president.

The company made the conventional glass products of the period—tableware, thermometer tubing and the like. Competition was fierce and in 1871 Amory Houghton, after losing a fortune, had to withdraw. The Corning works were sold to Nathan Cushing of Boston.

Under the new control, Amory Houghton, Jr., became manager of the plant. He shrewdly began to introduce specialized products. The new idea paid off and after a tough struggle he had the business back on its feet. On the formation of the Corning Glass Works in 1875 he became its first president.

In 1879 Thomas A. Edison was looking for a suitable bulb for his newly invented incandescent lamp. He came to Corning and the glassmakers there finally made one to his satisfaction. Thus began electric bulb production, an important part of Corning Glass Works' far-flung business.

The company began developing new glasses with wider applications in commerce and industry. Its development in 1908 of a heat-resistant glass gave railroaders a signal lantern globe that withstood sudden temperature changes without breaking. In 1915 Pyrex, heat-resistant ovenware, a boon to the housewife, was evolved. That was followed by other new heat-resistant products, many of them important to science.

In 1926 came the ribbon machine which makes as many glass bulbs in one minute as a two-man team of expert glass-blowers could turn out in eight hours. That same year of 1926 the last of eight chimneys, towering over the factories along the Chemung, went down. Automatic production had succeeded hand-made operations. Only in the manufacture of artistic glass doors the old hand craftsmanship still prevail. But in glass making, it takes a skilled workman to handle the machines.

An important date in Corning's glass-making calendar was the founding in 1903 of the Steuben Glass plant by Frederick Carder, a young English sculptor who had observed the making of art glass in Vienna. In 1904 the term, Crystal City, was first applied to Corning.

But after the acquisition of the Steuben plant by Corning Glass in 1918, the demand for art glass fell off and the directors considered abandoning its manufacture. Into the picture stepped young Arthur A. Houghton, Jr., a great-grandson of the first Amory, just out of Harvard. In his make-up the artistic and the practical are nicely blended. He proposed a revolutionary change in the manufacture of Steubenware. Previously the glass blowers had designed their own pieces. Houghton proposed the making of uniform designs by professional artists. The experiment was a decided success, both financially and artistically.

Cut glass and artistic glassware have been made in Corning for a long time. John Hoare opened a shop in 1868 and in the reign of General Grant furnished glass to the White House. In 1880 T. G. Hawkes founded the company which still bears his name and which has filled orders for cut glass for two Presidents, Cleveland and McKinley. The Hunt Glass Works, founded in 1895 and still in operation, was commissioned by President Harding in 1920 to supply hundreds of stemware items.

In October, 1947, Corning was again in the news when President Truman chose a Steuben crystal piece, the "Merry Go Round," as a wedding gift for Princess Elizabeth of England. And that same year Corning Glass duplicated a rare glass sanctuary lamp for use at the Holy Sepulcher in Jerusalem.

But the most spectacular chapter in the long history of glass making in the Crystal City was written in 1934. The eyes of the world were focused on Corning where the Glass Works was making the largest piece of glass in all history. It was a 200-inch telescope mirror disk for the Hale telescope to be mounted at the Mount Palomar Observatory in California.

After three years of experimentation and work in a domed observatory, specially built for the purpose in Centerway Square, the first disk, poured in March, 1934, was found to be imperfect. Some of the cores broke loose because of the intense heat of the molten glass. So it had to be done all over again.

The second mirror was completed in December, 1934. This time there was no flaw. The huge glass was carefully loaded on special cars for the trip to the Pacific Coast. The second World War prevented its installation on the mountain top until June of 1948.

The first giant disk, the imperfect one, is on display at the Corning Glass Center, about the first thing to meet the visitor's eye. What other industry has so effectively dramatized a failure?

The Corning Glass Center, a fabulous place, was dedicated in May, 1951, in celebration of the centennial of the company. Governor Dewey was principal speaker at the ceremony. Held in connection with the opening of the Center was a world conference of leaders in social science, industry and labor, under the general theme, "Living in an Industrial Civilization."

The Center houses the world's most complete library on glass, as well as the largest collection of historical glassware, ranging from the 20-ton disk in the lobby to a tiny Egyptian amphoriskos of about 1500 B.C., which was made by winding glass paste around a central core. The Center also provides a meeting place and all sorts of recreational facilities for company employees. It also serves as a community auditorium.

A highlight of a visit to the Center is crossing a bridge made of glass tubing on a steel foundation and entering the Steuben plant from the exhibit halls. There fine art is blown and shaped in processes centuries old and polished and engraved by master craftsmen. All this the visitor can watch from galleries above.

The visitor watches a workman plunge a hollow rod into the pot or crucible in the furnace. The melted glass clings to the end. By waving and blowing in the tube, it is elongated and through the skill of the craftsman, it is manipulated into the required form and pressed into shape. Red hot metal is worked in making the handles of pitchers and lamps. The product goes into a brick oven for annealing, is cooled gradually, then is inspected and packed.

The Glass Center and the Steuben Works form the showplace of the industry. Strung along the river and in the heart of town are eight other Corning plants of the company. They produce, to name a few items, electric light bulbs, radio tubes, cooking utensils, experimental glass, optical and chemical ware.

Corning Glass has plants in nine other cities, including Bradford and Wellsboro, over the Pennsylvania line. The one in Wellsboro makes Christmas tree ornaments and bulbs.

In the Glass Works files are 50,000 formulae which have produced 37,000 separate products. Among them is glass strong enough to serve as piping in steel mills; so soft it can be melted with a match; so resistant to thermal shock it can be heated a cherry red and then doused in ice water without cracking or breaking.

Four generations of the Houghton family have been associated with the industry that Amory, Sr., founded in 1851. Amory, Jr. was its savior in the 1870s. In the third generation were Arthur A. and Alanson B., the latter a onetime ambassador to Germany and Great Britain, an unsuccessful Republican candidate for the United States Senate and one of Steuben's most famous sons. Carrying on the tradition is the third Amory, now chairman of the board of Corning Glass, and Arthur A. Jr., head of the Steuben Works.

The Houghtons are unpretentious people, not given to self aggrandizement, yet leaders in their community. The present Amory Houghton's mansion, finest residence in the city, is perched on the side of the highest hill above the Crystal City. Characteristically he calls it "The Knoll."

The president of Corning Glass is William Decker. General Walter Bedell Smith is a director of the company. Heading the large research staff is Dr. Edward Condon, former director of the National Bureau of Standards, whose defense of the rights of scientists made news a few years ago. A venerated figure is Dr. Eugene C. Sullivan, honorary chairman of the board and Corning's "Grand Old Man of Research."

Generations of the same family have worked for Corning

Glass. Some of the veteran gaffers (gaffer is an old English word for head of the shop) came from Germany and Scandanavia. People of many racial strains work and live in the Crystal City. They are all Americans.

It might be worthy of mention that the Glass Works has 9,000 employees on its Corning payroll. That is half the population of the city.

* * *

Despite its industrialization—or maybe because of it—Corning supports cultural activities on a scale unusual for a city of its size. It has its own philharmonic and symphony orchestras, which give concerts in the Glass Center. Its Little Theater group, the Workshop Players, presents weekly plays. The Arena Players of Rochester provided a Summer theater in 1953. There is a community choral group which gives traditional concerts at Thanksgiving and Easter.

The presence of so many scientists and glass company executives, along with the high type of skilled labor in the Crystal City, account in part for its cultural advantages.

Corning has produced, along with its giant mirrors and crystal goblets, some remarkable men and women. One was red-headed Maggie Higgins, born in 1883 to a free-thinking Irish stonecutter father and a tubercular mother. She was one of 11 children. Mike Higgins was the first and at one time the only Socialist in the village. When Robert G. Ingersoll, the silver tongued agnostic, spoke in Corning, Mike escorted him to the meeting hall, heedless of muttered threats along the line.

It is little wonder that his daughter, Maggie, became the founder and world leader of the birth control movement, was jailed and scorned for that cause and other unconventional "isms."

When Margaret Sanger came to write her autobiography and her thoughts turned back to the village where she was born, she remembered first of all the steep hills and wrote: "The streets of Corning, N. Y., where I was born climb right up from the Chemung River which cuts the town in two. ... The people who live there have floppy knees from going up and down."

Corning was the home of another celebrity—in a different field. He was John Comosh, circus acrobat famed for his feat in completing the triple somersault four times. He was the only man in history to do it more than once. Born in Corning in 1854, he ran away at the age of eight and joined a circus. He joined the Portuguese Worland family of acrobats and took their name. He traveled with P. T. Barnum, with Dan Rice and Adam Forepaugh and was a crony of Buffalo Bill. On his retirement in 1889 he turned to the prosaic business of selling coal in his home town until his death in 1933.

Through the years Corning has often felt the anger of the floodwaters of the Chemung and Monkey Run. In 1859 it was "the pumpkin flood," so called because when the swollen streams swept over thousands of acres, thousands of pumpkins, washed out of the corn fields, floated past Corning on the crest of the waters.

In 1889 came the "million dollar flood." A child was drowned and many families had to flee their homes. In 1896 the state built a dike along the Chemung but in 1935 the same flood that smote Hornell did enormous damage in Corning.

Since then Uncle Sam has built other dikes to check the Chemung and a project to tame the Monkey Run is now in the government hopper.

On July 4, 1912 Gibson, on the outskirts of Corning, was the scene of one of Upstate New York's greatest disasters. It was in the early morning and the first section of a Lackawanna passenger train was stalled by a freight train with a broken draw head. Roaring through the fog at 65 miles an hour, the second section of the express ploughed into the stalled train. Two coaches at the rear were telescoped and every passenger in them was killed. The total death toll was 41.

Oldest building standing in Corning is the former Jennings tavern at 58 West Pulteney Street. The rambling, dignified old inn, painted white and with green blinds, was built in 1796 by Charles Williamson, the land agent. For a time Ben Patterson, the Daniel Boone of the Southern Tier, kept tavern there. It now is an apartment house.

Other landmarks of the Crystal City:

The clock tower in the square that is a memorial to Erastus Corning, founder of the city. It was erected in 1889 by the grandchildren of the Albany grandee. A local builder fashioned it of the native Antrim stone and the clock in its tower was made by a noted French craftsman.

The gray stone building with its medieval towers and turrets peeping over the trees on the hill along West First Street. It was built as a state arsenal in 1858 and later became a Catholic home for destitute children.

The Corning Public Library, a noble, pillared structure, which is a World War I memorial and which contains an art glass window designed by Frederick Carder, said to be worth $30,000 and the only one of its kind in the world.

The spacious Memorial Stadium, erected in memory of the heroes of the second World War and dedicated during the Corning Centennial of 1948, with a general named

Eisenhower as the principal speaker. There the Corning entry in the PONY League holds forth.

*   *   *

Southwest of Corning is the picturesque old village of Addison on the Canisteo River. Travelers will remember the place named after the English essayist for the Victorian Fire Hall, five stories high, that stands at the bend of Route 17, and for the 130-year-old American Hotel, with its post-colonial architecture.

The old Addison Academy is gone. Its most famous student was a lad named Tom Watson, the son of a lumberman over in Dry Run, in the Town of Campbell. Watson senior wanted his son to go to college and study law. But Tom, after quitting the Academy at the age of 17, settled for a year at the Elmira School of Commerce. The business world, not Blackstone, beckoned him.

He sold pianos, sewing machines and organs and installed a double entry system of bookkeeping at a store in Painted Post before he started selling cash registers at the age of 19. The boy from Dry Run went on to head International Business Machines, to be called "the king of salesmen," and to become one of America's best known captains of industry.

Thomas J. Watson in his time has received a score of honorary degrees and the decorations of foreign nations. But his real Alma Maters are Addison Academy, the Elmira School of Commerce and the "University of Experience."

Before the Civil War, a celebrated homespun politician named Andrew Bray Dickinson, "Old Bray" they called him, kept store on his father's farm at Hornby Flats, northeast of Corning. He was a power in the Whig Party.

In the 1850s "Old Bray" went to Illinois to drive a herd of cattle back home to Steuben and in Springfield he met a homely, gangling lawyer named Lincoln. After Abraham Lincoln was elected president, Dickinson sent him a letter in an execrable scrawl, asking for the job of marshal in the Western New York district.

Lincoln passed the letter around at a cabinet meeting in the hope somebody could decipher it. Secretary of War Stanton said: "It's perfectly plain. The man wants to be minister to Nicaragua." So Lincoln named his friend to the diplomatic post. "Old Bray" spent three weeks in a hotel room in Washington, learning Spanish from a tutor.

He made an excellent minister and stayed at the post in Nicaragua until he died. The grateful people of that country erected a monument to the memory of "Old Bray" of Steuben.

Arch Merrill's New York

Twenty-three volumes comprise the series of regional history and folklore created by Arch Merrill from the 1940s through the 1960s.

Watch for additional volumes of the series at your favorite bookstore or send a postal card and request to be placed on our mailing list for notification as future titles are released.

Empire State Books
a division of
Heart of the Lakes Publishing
PO Box 299
Interlaken, NY 14847